BARRICADES

The First African-American West Point Cadets
and Their Constant Fight for Survival

TOM CARHART

Copyright © 2020 by Thomas Merritt Carhart III.

Library of Congress Control Number:		2020906999
ISBN:	Hardcover	978-1-7960-9742-9
	Softcover	978-1-7960-9741-2
	eBook	978-1-7960-9740-5

All rights reserved. No part of this book may be reproduced or transmitted in any form or by any means, electronic or mechanical, including photocopying, recording, or by any information storage and retrieval system, without permission in writing from the copyright owner.

Cover Illustration Courtesy of the Library of Congress Prints and Photographs Division: West Point viewed from the Hudson River in the early 1820s. Painted by W.G. Wall and engraved by John Hill. Portraits of Alexander, Flipper and Young: Courtesy of Elaine McConnell, Librarian, and the U.S. Military Academy at West Point.
Illustration of James Smith: Courtesy of the New York Public Library.
Illustration of Johnson Whittiker: Courtesy of the New York Historical Society.

Any people depicted in stock imagery provided by Getty Images are models, and such images are being used for illustrative purposes only.
Certain stock imagery © Getty Images.

Print information available on the last page.

Rev. date: 05/29/2020

To order additional copies of this book, contact:
Xlibris
1-888-795-4274
www.Xlibris.com
Orders@Xlibris.com
811438

For Jan

Other Books by Tom Carhart

Battles and Campaigns in Vietnam (Crown, 1984)

The Offering (Vietnam memoir -- Morrow, 1987)

Iron Soldiers (Pocket Books, 1994)

West Point Warriors (Warner, 2002)

Still Loyal Be (Bettim Press, 2003)

Lost Triumph (Putnam, 2005)

Sacred Ties (Berkley Caliber, 2010)

The Golden Fleece (Potomac Books, 2017)

Contents

Introduction ix

Chapter 1	West Point in the 19th Century 1
Chapter 2	African-Americans and Military Service 17
Chapter 3	The First Black Cadets 27
Chapter 4	Henry Ossian Flipper 49
Chapter 5	Johnson Chesnut Whittaker 67
Chapter 6	The Fight Endures 93
Chapter 7	John Hanks Alexander 123
Chapter 8	Charles Young 137
Chapter 9	A Mixed Record 149

Bibliography 157
Appendix A 169
Appendix B 173

INTRODUCTION

These are powerful, even heart-rending stories, strongly affected by the racism of the era. Yet they must be told, for despite contemporary racial issues, these stories have given rise to the modern U.S. Army in which African American West Point graduates can aspire to full Army careers, even to the stars of a general.

During the years 1870-1887, 27 young men who formally represented themselves as having some African American ancestry were nominated for appointment to West Point. Apparently, these were the only African Americans appointed during the nineteenth century, although it is difficult to know for certain, since the War Department did not maintain separate records for them.

In a letter of February 9, 1898, Titus N. Alexander of the Detroit Tribune asked the Secretary of War to send him the names of "Negroes" appointed to West Point up until that date. In his reply, the Adjutant General stated:

> The War Department has kept no record of the colored cadets separate from the white; nor do the nominations, or appointments, of cadets make any distinction in that respect. The Department is therefore unable to inform you of the actual number, etc., of colored youths appointed as cadets; but it is believed that 12 colored cadets have been admitted to the U.S. Military Academy.[1]

In the nineteenth century there was no formal way in which the race of a cadet candidate would have been conveyed to West Point before his arrival. However, given the publicity attaching to some members of congress who were seeking a qualified black to nominate and the fact that the army is part of the federal government, it is probable that West Point got early notice of the anticipated arrival of many, if not all, of the blacks nominated for appointment. But this is only true for those whose appearance betrayed their race. If a cadet candidate was only 1/4 or 1/8 black and was particularly light-skinned and white-looking, unless he acknowledged his race, there was no formal way for anyone at West Point to learn that he was, under the standards of the time, "black." This was an issue of some importance for cadets Johnson Whittaker and William Hare, whose experiences will be discussed in chapters to follow.

In 1899, this changed somewhat, as cadet candidates were required to fill out forms that attempted to accumulate certain personal information. This included such things as the amount of previous schooling a cadet candidate had had, his use of tobacco, and the nationality of his parents. Most white cadets simply filled in the nationality blanks with "American," except in the obvious cases of parents who had a different nationality. But on June 14, 1918, cadet candidate John Byron Alexander filled in the blanks after "Father" and "Mother" with the words "Afro-American," thus formally acknowledging his race.[2]

A list of the 27 African American nominees to West Point, the source by name of Representative, Congressional District, and state, along with the outcome of their nominations to West Point, is found at Appendix A. A list of the twelve who were admitted, the dates of their arrivals and departures and the cause of their departures is found at Appendix B. Six of the twelve failed academically at the end of their first semester; one more failed after his first year; two completed three and a half years of study before failing academically (though both had been required to repeat one year, and were therefore in their "Second Class," or Junior year when they were dismissed on academic grounds) and three graduated.

My approach has been to open with short chapters that will introduce the reader to West Point as it was in the nineteenth century, to the experience of black Americans serving in military roles, and white perceptions of blacks in the nineteenth century. I will then look at black cadets sequentially as they arrived at West Point, follow their experiences over time, and attempt thereby to measure their progress in the larger society governed by its white majority. I will attempt to observe them first as individuals, but also as members of the same social caste: the descendants of slaves.

It is hoped that this will allow the reader to see and understand some important things about American society and the way it has changed over time, aspects of American history about which they might otherwise be largely ignorant.

The Civil War profoundly changed our nascent nation in many ways. But in the lives of those Americans born in bondage, the most important outcome was the end of slavery and their consequent freedom. And the immediate differences that meant were quite profound: for the first time, former slaves were allowed to travel freely, to acquire education, to enter the marketplace and engage in contracts. And most important, at least in theory: they had won the right to vote.

But those freedoms were illusory, and after Reconstruction, most former slaves found themselves still living agricultural subsistence lives in a sharecropping economy with no end or exit in sight. So how were they supposed to get ahead? Where was the "American Dream" for them?

Access to a higher station in life always seemed to require education, a fact that limited the progress out of peonage for many former slaves. That was especially true in any of the respected professional fields, some of which embodied whole intellectual worlds and, for maximum effect, required education from the "right" schools.

One such widely respected professional field during the nineteenth century was the military. And once again, there was a "right" school: The United States Military Academy at West Point, New York.

Given the grinding subordinate roles they filled in society, there are few celebratory stories from the late nineteenth century about the stellar behavior of individual African Americans rising to meet harsh challenges as young adults. But here is one such set of stories, of young black men who won political appointments to West Point, then endured the most cruel and callous treatment from their contemporaries as they fought to win their diplomas. Early on, most of the dozen who showed up fell by the wayside academically. But for however long they lasted, black cadets were all routinely cut off socially from their white peers, and those three who made it and graduated did so, to use their own terminology, by "standing on each other's shoulders".

These stories are coarse and brutal. And while the extra challenges faced by the first African American cadets at West Point were very real, their positions are readily understandable today, and their behavior, ultimately, was quite wonderful. They are worthy role models today, not only for West Point cadets, but for all young Americans.

ENDNOTES: Introduction

1. Adjutant General to Titus N. Alexander, Feb. 25, 1898, File 137 o. M.A. 1898, Correspondence Relating to the U.S. Military Academy, 1867-1904, Records of the Adjutant General's Office, 1780's-1917, Record Group 94, National Archives, Washington, D.C
2. Record Group 404, Series 189, "Personal and School History Sheets of Cadet Candidates, 1899-1947", U.S. Military Academy Archives, West Point, N.Y.

Chapter I

West Point in the 19th Century

If there is to be any chance of understanding just what it was like for the first African-Americans to attend West Point in the 19th century, we need to know what West Point itself was like at the time, as well as the roles of African-Americans in the U.S. Army. Many well-informed readers will know that one Sylvanus Thayer, an early superintendent, is regarded as "the Father of West Point" because of the rigid military academy structure that he there established. Others may also be dimly aware that some African-Americans serving in the U.S. Army were known as "buffalo soldiers" during the Indian Wars in the West. Aside from a few random facts such as those, however, few will have given much thought to the society that these first African-Americans confronted when they attempted to become officers in the US Army. This widely-respected professional field was its own society, still deeply influenced by the attitudes that had supported, or at least tolerated, centuries of slavery.

As for the history of West Point, the first surprise may be that arguably the true Father of West Point was none other than the Father of Our Country—George Washington—although Alexander Hamilton deserves credit for drawing up the first plan for such an academy. Its origins actually lie in the Revolutionary War, when a great need was felt on the American side for trained, competent military figures. Raw courage often sufficed for men to fight effectively in infantry and cavalry units, but for any field army to operate effectively, technical expertise was essential in the key fields of engineering and artillery. Since there were no formal military schools on this side of the Atlantic, and men born in this country had seen little large-scale combat, there was limited native technical skill in the Continental Army. The presence of European military experts who filled key roles in American ranks, men like Steuben and Kosciusko and Lafayette, made the need all the more apparent.

The Continental Army's commanding general, George Washington, did the best he could, and after the peace treaty was signed in 1783, he called for "academies, one or more, for the instruction of the art military." Washington declared: "I cannot conclude without repeating the necessity of the proposed Institution, unless we intend to let the Science [of war] become extinct, and to depend entirely upon the Foreigners for their friendly aid."[1]

Nothing came of this, though many prominent Americans agreed with Washington's conception. Finally, in 1799, Alexander Hamilton gave a detailed plan for an academy to Secretary of War James McHenry, and sent a copy to Washington. In the last letter he ever wrote, on 1 December 1799, two days before his death, Washington told Hamilton the establishment of such an institution "has ever been considered by me as an object of primary importance to this country," and said he hoped Hamilton's arguments would "prevail upon the Legislature to place it on a permanent and respectable footing."[2]

In January 1800, President John Adams presented Hamilton's basic plan to Congress. They deliberated and did nothing, as Congresses sometimes do. Finally, Thomas Jefferson acted in May 1801, when he had the army begin preparations for the establishment of a military academy at West Point, New York. In March, 1802, Congress finally passed legislation establishing both a corps of engineers and a military academy at West Point. The academy opened officially that July.[3]

But a political divide had started a decade earlier, in 1791-1792, between the Federalists and the Republicans. In 1798, fears of American involvement in a European war grew, and the incumbent Federalists used such fears to their advantage by, among other things, expanding the military. Republicans feared that this larger force would be used primarily to silence their political opposition, and the passage of the Alien and Sedition Acts seemed to bear them out. But the election of Jefferson in 1800 ended the looming crisis, and he began work immediately to reduce the size and potential threat of the enlarged army.

How could Jefferson support a military academy while also leading his party's clear opposition to a large, standing military? The explanation from most historians who have addressed the issue is that they have found Jefferson's position on a national military academy to be an extension of his support for a national university that emphasized the study of science.[4] The best answer may be that given in *Mr. Jefferson's Army* by Theodore Crackel,[5] in which he holds that Jefferson personally was not at all opposed to the existence of a professional army per se, but rather only to the American army that existed at the time, and then only because of the Federalist political sentiments of its leadership. At the outset of his presidency, more than 90% of the officers in the army were Federalist political opponents of Jefferson. As a function of his careful reorganization of the army's officer corps so as to discharge his hidebound political enemies, convert the less zealous to his cause, and infuse the force with the fresh blood of his loyalists, by 1809 the numbers had reversed so that fully 90% of the officers were then his political supporters. Jefferson had slowly and carefully changed the very political nature of the army's leadership, and he saw a military academy at West Point as a powerful tool by which he could train and commission as officers of his army the sons of loyal Republicans and help to politically reform the army from within.[6]

In his attempt to establish a military academy that would train politically selected young men from across the nation, Jefferson was taking bold steps, and early success should not have been expected. Indeed, for the first fifteen years of its existence, the structural, political, and organizational problems confronted by the new military academy caused it to be of only minimal value to the leadership of the army it was intended to serve.

President James Madison, Jefferson's Republican successor, called in 1815 for adequate military and naval forces in peacetime, direct taxation, and a national bank -- things the Republican Party had previously loudly opposed. But by this time, the Republicans no longer feared that the Federalists, whose national political power had faded badly, posed a genuine threat to individual freedoms, and the personal political inclinations of army officers were no longer the central issue to the nation's leadership that they had been.

In 1817, President James Monroe appointed Major Sylvanus Thayer, a graduate of both Dartmouth (1807) and West Point (1808), as the Superintendent. Thayer first went to France, where he studied and collected materials at the prestigious Ecole Polytechnique. Formal education in the sciences was sorely lacking in the United States, so Thayer was sent to France primarily to accumulate the best materials and experience available in military and engineering fields, that these might be applied in his new post and so dramatically raise the quality of the U.S. Military Academy.

The recently founded (1794) Ecole Polytechnique had a rigid curriculum based on mathematics and science applied with rigor and uniformity. And it was effective: the Ecole Polytechnique produced France's best engineers, mathematicians, government administrators, and military officers. After the better part of a year of study there, Thayer returned to the United States and assumed his new post as Superintendent of the U.S. Military Academy at West Point, New York.

Thayer immediately established at the Academy both new standards of rigid discipline as well as a new system of education. He set up the Academic Board, which consisted of the heads of the various academic departments, and together they established a rigorous four-year curriculum of studies that was primarily focused on engineering, but also included chemistry, physics, history, geography, law, and ethics. The academic "weeding out" of the less competent began right away.[7]

One of Thayer's key academic innovations was small classroom sections of perhaps a dozen cadets per teacher, with each cadet required to recite part of the day's assigned lesson and receive a grade for that recitation on every day on which class was held - an almost sacrosanct tradition that endures to the present in some subject areas. He also set up a constantly updated ranking, by academic grades, in each of the four year-group "classes" at the Academy at any given time, with praise and other plums passed out to those at the top of the heap. This evolved to the point that choice of assignment in the army upon graduation and commissioning of each cadet was long selected as a function of their general "order of merit" in a given class,[8] a practice that endures to this day in modified format.

Thayer dramatically changed both West Point as an institution and the quality of the education of its graduates. He was to remain the Superintendent until 1833, when President Andrew Jackson's personal displeasure with him brought about his resignation. But parts of both his disciplinary and educational systems remain in place at West Point to this very day, and that is why he is revered as the "Father of the Military Academy."[9]

From the beginning, cadets had been appointed to West Point by the Secretary of War, often with one appointment being made from each congressional district and with the selection turning on the recommendation of the Congressional Representative from that district, but with no legal format. In 1843, Congress passed legislation that established the process for appointment of cadets to West Point, one from each congressional district, and ten appointments for the President. These presidential appointments went to the sons of career officers, men who had generally lost their political bases when they entered the service of their country - often the only possible way for West Point graduates who spent their careers in the military to send their sons to West Point.[10]

The attainment of an appointment to West Point by a young man, however, has always had a political aspect. Although the Republican-Federalist rivalry and its effect on which young man obtained a given appointment disappeared early, the ability of Members of Congress to control appointments was in and of itself quite political. Some Members, from the early days, remained aloof from the decision of whom to nominate and depended on free and open competition among applicants within their congressional districts on specific tests. But this has never been a requirement: All that was required was the submission of a name - the nomination - of an individual of appropriate age and gender[11] from the district of the Member of Congress who wanted to go to West Point, with no other specification. Some Members of Congress, therefore, have intruded personally and selected someone to receive the nomination for appointment for purely personal or political reasons and with no reference to the merit of that individual relative to other applicants. Under the law, that is their complete right, for standards by which a nominee is to be selected from among a pool of applicants are nowhere specified for Members of Congress.

Consequently, for a would-be applicant, this usually meant writing letters to his Congressional Representative requesting consideration for an appointment to West Point. Simultaneously, he tried to get someone influential to recommend him to that Member of Congress. But many more letters and recommendations would be required, usually over a period of many months or even years.

A good example of the steps required can be seen by examining the case of Henry O. Flipper, who in 1877 became the first African American to graduate from West Point. In his autobiographical account of his time at West Point, he sets down the steps he took to obtain a nomination. In October, 1872, Flipper decided that, if a Republican were elected to Congress from the district of Georgia .in which he lived, then he would apply for appointment to West Point. It turned out that Republican J.C. Freeman was elected, and Flipper immediately requested his support. In his West Point memoir, he reprints the six consecutive letters he received from Congressman Freeman as he slowly worked his way through the maze of securing a nomination to West Point. The first letter, dated 23 January 1873, includes the following key section:

You are a stranger to me and before I can comply with your request you must get your teacher, Mr. James L. Dunning, P.M., Colonel H.P. Fanorr, and other Republicans to indorse for you. Give me assurance you are worthy and well qualified and I will recommend you." [12]

The second letter, dated 22 March 1873, acknowledges having heard from Flipper and indicates that Freeman has been invited by the War Department to nominate a legally qualified young man from his District for an appointment to West Point. It continues:

> As you were the first applicant, I am disposed to give you the first chance; but the requirements are rigid and strict, and I think you had best come down and see them. If after reading them you think you can undergo the examination without doubt, I will nominate you. But I do not want my nominee to fail to get in.[13]

It would seem, at this point, that, if any political endorsement or other assurance was required from third parties by Freeman, that has been received, for he says he is prepared to nominate Flipper. The third letter, dated 26 March, 1873, contains the following:

> While your education may be sufficient, it requires many other qualifications - such as age, height, form, etc.; soundness of lungs, limbs, etc. I will send you the requirements, if you desire them, and call upon three competent gentlemen to examine you, if you desire it.[14]

While Freeman had said in the previous letter that he was ready to nominate Flipper, things seem to have somehow changed, for Freeman now begins to specify what will be expected of Flipper before he can be nominated. But Flipper stayed the course, and the fourth letter, dated 28 March, 1873, includes the following:

> I have concluded too send the paper sent me to J. A. Holtzclaw, of Atlanta, present Collector of Internal Revenue. You can call on him and examine for yourself. If you then

think you can pass, I will designate three men to examine you, and if they pronounce you up to the requirements, I will appoint you.[15]

More hurdles, but Flipper remains undeterred. The fifth letter, dated 5 April, 1873, presents the first unalloyed good news:

> The board of examiners pronounce you qualified to enter the Military Academy at West Point will appoint you, and send on the papers to the Secretary of War, who will notify you of the same. From his letter to me you will have to be at West Point by the 25t h day of May, 1873.[16]

This was the good news for which Flipper had been waiting. And his last letter from Freeman before he entered West Point, dated 17 April 1873, still left him options:

> I this day inclose you papers from the war Department. You can carefully read and then make up your mind whether you accept the position assigned you. If you should sign up, direct and forward to proper authorities, Washington, D.C.[17]

The papers were three: a letter from the Secretary of War informing Flipper that he had been conditionally selected for appointment as a cadet at the United States Military Academy, and two longer lists of medical, academic, and physical requirements for admission to West Point, for which requirements he would be tested as part of the formal admission process. Flipper accepted his nomination, passed the admissions tests, and graduated in 1877.

The admission standards against which Flipper was measured in 1873 were quite rigorous, but this had not always been the case. During much of the nineteenth century, many Members of Congress, particularly those from the western and southern parts of the country where education of the young was limited, were unhappy to see so many of their nominees turned away at the very gates of West Point because they were unable to meet the admission standards. They wanted the standards lowered, that their nominees might be admitted, educated, and ultimately graduate. As a function of this expressed

Congressional concern, the standards required of nominees for passage of the admission tests varied; sometimes, the tests were not terribly difficult.

West Point would survive political attacks by President Andrew Jackson and his allies, who called it an "elitist" institution in the 1830s. But by then, it had begun to play an important role no other institution in the nation could play, a role Jackson and every other leader in the nation, had they truly considered matters, almost certainly would have wanted it to continue to play. That role was the production of well-trained civil engineers, men who established the initial communication and transportation grids for the expanding nation: harbors, railroads, bridges, highways, canals, the great bulk of which were built and/or improved by West Point graduates. West Point was the only source of civil engineers who had been classroom educated in the United States during the early nineteenth century, and West Point graduates were the first teachers in the scientific schools later established at Harvard and Yale.[18]

The period from 1840 until 1860 has often been referred to as West Point's "Golden Age." Before its graduates were called on to perform the military tasks for which they were being trained, its engineering preeminence was renowned. Textbooks written by West Point faculty dominated the fields of mathematics, chemistry, and engineering. Francis Wayland, Brown University's President, said, "The single academy at West Point has done more toward the construction of railroads than all our colleges united."[19]

Then in April 1846, President James K. Polk baited the Mexican army into crossing the Rio Grande and attacking American troops, thus justifying his "defensive" war in response. Polk was certain the U.S. Army would handle the war with ease, which would allow him to pressure Mexico into the sale of California by force of arms[20]

There were a few bloody battles fought in Mexico, and the U.S. Army won them all. West Point had not yet established itself in the upper ranks of the army, and it had produced none of the generals in this war. But many young graduates served as junior officers, and nearly all the West Pointers who would rise to high command on both sides in the American Civil War were blooded here: Robert E. Lee, Ulysses S. Grant, .George B. McClellan, Jefferson Davis, and many more - their names and feats on other days would one day ring loud and help to spread the fame of West Point around the world.[21]

General Winfield Scott, the commander of American forces, was not himself a West Point graduate, but he had this to say about West Point graduates serving in the war. "I give it as my fixed opinion that, but for our graduated cadets, the war between the United States and Mexico might, and probably would have, lasted some four or five years, with, in its first half, more defeats than victories falling to our share; whereas, in less than two campaigns, we conquered a great country and a peace, without the loss of a single battle or skirmish."[22]

After the end of the Mexican American war, West Point had established itself in the national consciousness not only as a school of civil engineering, but also as the source of military training for the officer corps that would lead American citizen-soldiers in war - its initial purpose and justification. Originally, Washington, Adams and Jefferson had all intended the Academy at West Point to train a cohort of young American men who would thereupon return to their home states and apply their military talents in their local militia, without expecting the graduates to join the regular forces and serve as professional soldiers. But that was never to be, partly because of the militia (the acquisition of a commission in a given state militia at the time often involved more in the way of naked bribery and payoffs than did a commission in the Regulars), partly because of failures on the part of West Point.[23]

Academic demands in the West Point classrooms remained rigorous, but this was to be the source of problems on Capitol Hill for the academy. In return for the 1843 act specifying the method of appointment to West Point and granting the "at large" appointments, Congress insisted that the entrance standards not be raised, so that young men of lower education from the South and West might also have access to a West Point education. But with the rigid curriculum, typically fewer than half of those admitted would graduate: in the class of 1859, for instance, from among 103 admitted, only 41 graduated.[24]

Thus, while admission standards were kept relatively low, the academic demands were such that only those young men who were either exceptionally bright or had been well prepared by a demanding education were able to survive. A disproportionate number of southerners and westerners were found deficient in their studies (or were simply "Found" in cadet slang) and dismissed. The result was that northeasterners who had been adequately educated before West Point tended to do well there academically. Since only those who stood high in their class at graduation were returned to serve as instructors or assistant professors, then ultimately become professors, the faculty was also heavily weighted with easterners: in 1840, all the professors were from the East, as were fourteen of the seventeen instructors and assistant professors.[25]

At Christmas 1860, there was great political turmoil loose in the land as some states seceded and others were pressured, from within and without, to follow suit or to forebear from so doing. The confusion at West Point was as great as it could have been anywhere in the nation, with so many cadets having been appointed there by Members of Congress from states now caught up in secessionist fever. After the attack on Fort Sumter, the Southern exodus really started, and by May, 65 of the 86 southerners at West Point, out of a total of 278 cadets, had resigned. Superintendent Bowman was convinced that the other 21 were waiting for their States to secede, at which time they would resign, so he forced all cadets to sign an oath of allegiance. All 21 signed.[26]

The Civil War was the one in which West Pointers clearly made their marks. In 55 of the 60 most significant battles, West Pointers commanded both sides, and in two of the other five, a West Pointer commanded one side. In the Union army, a total of 294 West Point graduates attained the rank of general in either the regulars or the volunteers, including three generals, one lieutenant general, 85 major generals, and 205 brigadier generals. In the Confederate army, the West Point graduates who reached the rank of general reached 151, including eight generals, 15 lieutenant generals, 48 major generals, and 88 brigadier generals.[27]

When the fanfare and celebration that attended the end of the Civil War had died down, West Point returned to a somewhat complacent normalcy, with no major war awaiting its graduates. Given the nature of the profession for which the Academy was preparing its students, there was at least some modest depression of mood among the student body, and perhaps the staff and faculty as well, in the wake of such a major war--a war that had been a major force in the growth of education, the increase in man's knowledge, and development of new technologies. The rapidity of change in Gilded Age America was dramatic, and new methods, new approaches, new ideas were as much a part of academia as any other part of the nation.

Before the Civil War, West Point had been an important forward-looking institution, key to the development of engineering schools at other major American colleges. But after the Civil War, as the volunteers were emptied out of the army and it was dramatically diminished in size and national importance, West Point drew in on itself protectively. The Thayer system of classroom education had been tried and proven; nothing new was needed. West Point cadets continued to be taught the same things, from the same textbooks, and for prolonged periods by the same people. All of West Point's staff and faculty (almost all of whom, after the Civil War and until 1900, had either taught there through its duration or were actively engaged in its prosecution) were drawn from among graduates of the academy. Any calls that might have been made for change at West Point were seen, both at the Academy and among the wider public, to be challenges, and these were quickly answered: the institution that had produced Grant and Sherman and Lee and Jackson had obviously found the correct way to train soldiers. As an academic and intellectual institution, however, West Point began to exhibit signs of impending suffocation.[28]

Meanwhile, to cadets at West Point, daily life was filled not only with academics, but also with the heavy hand of military regulation: drill, guard mounts, more drill; the regular inspections of their rooms, possessions, and persons; and still more drill. The authorities at West Point were ever mindful that their responsibility went far beyond the simple education of a young man, but also extended to producing well-trained, well-disciplined novice officers who could apply their skills in the nation's army. And whatever the relative value of the academic education imparted at West Point may have been, its primary purpose remained the production of the very best army officers. At West Point itself, the major issues in the latter part of the nineteenth century that were the greatest concern to the Army and to the public were hazing and black cadets. Black cadets are the main focus of this work, and the issues related to hazing are important to a full understanding of the situation they confronted.

Before the Civil War, new cadets arrived at West Point and went directly into a nearby summer camp where they lived in tents, practicing soldiery before classes began in the fall. Some hazing occurred then, but it was mostly harmless pranks that either embarrassed the newcomer or made him look silly. After the war, a new practice began: new cadets were assigned to rooms in the normal area of barracks at West Point where, before going to camp, they underwent three weeks of training in military fundamentals - marching, saluting, shining shoes, and so on. It was at this time that hazing appeared, and it lasted throughout the first, or "Plebe," year of these new cadets. Upperclassmen would make Plebes assume and hold strained positions, including exaggerated positions of attention known as "bracing"; eat or drink noxious substances; and engage in physically exhausting exercises.

If upperclassmen were particularly displeased with a given plebe, he would be "called out," or challenged to a bare knuckle fistfight by the upperclassmen. His opponent would be an upperclassman roughly his own size, but the purpose of such a fight was to give the plebe a good whipping, so tough opponents always appeared. If a plebe won a given fight, another upperclassman would "call him out" until, eventually, he had been put in his place.[29] The fights were formally staged, with a referee, a timekeeper for rounds, cadets to act as seconds for each fighter, and lookouts to watch for and warn of officers approaching who might discover the fight. Fights were explicitly forbidden, but again, enforcement by officers who were themselves graduates and had gone through the same rites of passage was unpredictable but generally lax. This hazing was forbidden by the rules, but at first it was largely ignored by the authorities and thus tolerated. And once classes of cadets had endured such practices as plebes, they wrought vengeance disguised as training on succeeding plebe classes. Superintendents occasionally became upset and worked hard to eliminate hazing, but their efforts were usually successful for only short periods. Yet in some incidents in the nineteenth century, cadet hazing involved physical injury. In one case, upperclassmen so "deviled" a plebe walking guard that he attacked them with his bayonet, piercing the thigh of one of his tormentors.[30] In another, a new plebe had his pants stripped off and was spread-eagled on the ground. While he was held in this position, other upperclassmen tied a string tight around his testicles and poured turpentine on his bare buttocks, causing severe pain and swelling.[31] And in 1871, one plebe was almost hanged, which left him with strained neck muscles and a painful rope burn.[32]

Eventually, earnest superintendents were able to control the more extreme forms of hazing. In the late nineteenth and early twentieth centuries, hazing was found not just at West Point, but was also well established at most civilian schools. The army was under great pressure from Congress to end the hazing at West Point, and military authorities attempted to satisfy Congress by eliminating the truly dangerous practices, and simply institutionalizing those that were little more than uncomfortable, explaining them as good military training.

As the hazing at West Point came under control, it endured for most of the twentieth century. Until the mid-1970s, plebes "braced" whenever they were outside their rooms but still within the "Area of Barracks," and during the summer of their arrival at West Point known as "Beast Barracks," they lived in a constant state of panic on a near-starvation diet. This regimen, intentionally difficult and demanding, was explained by Academy authorities as a way to condition new cadets with harshness: teach them how to act and react under pressure, how to learn to control themselves coolly when the external demands artificially placed on their shoulders might otherwise overwhelm them. While you cannot replicate combat, you can approximate its pressures in other ways, and practice under those conditions will allow better performance when the moment is at hand.

That explanation, of course, may be little more than rationalization. In the last two decades of the twentieth century, the harsh nature in which plebes had long been treated was dramatically lessened, and a more humane system of leadership development replaced it. During the nineteenth century, however, and up until the last quarter of the twentieth century, the hazing of plebes was a normal part of cadet life at West Point, and it was this tradition that confronted the first young black men at West Point.

After the end of the Civil War and the enactment of the Thirteenth Amendment and its implementing legislation, the civil rights of all African-Americans, whether former slaves or freedmen, were at least theoretically much the same as those of any white American. But in most circumstances, such legal provisions were generally of only limited effect. Longstanding customs and experiences were too strongly ingrained in social relations between the races to make much dramatic change in the short run possible.

The timeframe in which the first African-Americans attended West Point (and, in at least one instance, graduated to start serving in the US Army) is traditionally known as the Reconstruction Period, and it is generally conceded that it remains one of the most controversial phases in America's history—controversial both in its activities and in the interpretation of these activities. This Reconstruction Period is usually dated to 1865-1877 and is characterized by several features: the stationing of Federal troops in the former Confederate states; the election of numerous Blacks to public office (including 17 elected to the US Congress); and the role of the so-called carpetbaggers, Northerners who moved into the South to acquire land and power (60 of them were elected to Congress and 9 as governors). These and other developments led to various acts of violence against Blacks, from spontaneous mob killings to the organized violence perpetrated by the newly formed Ku Klux Klan. Even the presence of Federal troops failed to prevent most of these violent actions.

All this was going on, as indicated, in the immediate aftermath of the Civil War, but it was also accompanied by various actions that might have seemed to offer some hope to African-Americans. Congress passed the 14th Amendment, giving citizenship to all blacks and guaranteeing them the protection of all federal and state laws; it then required that the former Confederate states ratify the 14th amendment in order to rejoin the Union. Dominated by Republicans, Congress even impeached President Andrew

Johnson for his resistance to their policies, and although it failed by one vote to convict and remove him from office, the action served notice that the Republicans and their governments in the South were going to try to impose a more equitable society.

To some extent, they succeeded. In particular, they established public, tax-supported school systems in many Southern states—including schools for the newly freed Blacks. They attracted investment money from the North and provided financial aid to building railroads and new industries. Some African-Americans did manage to improve their status. Most Blacks, however, remained tied to the land, land still owned by whites, and so they were left laboring as "free men" on farms for their former masters. Gradually Democrats took over the state governments and at the same time the Federal troops slowly withdrew from the South. When Rutherford Hayes, a Republican, was tied in the election of 1876 with the Democrat, Samuel Tilden, he got Tilden to step aside by promising to remove the last remaining troops. Which he did on assuming office in 1877 and it is this act that historians regard as the end of the Reconstruction Period.

Underneath all these governmental actions, however, little was changing in "the hearts and minds" of most white Southerners—and for that matter, many Northerners. And with numerous exceptions, little would change for many decades after the end of Reconstruction. Even the abolitionists who had so stoutly opposed slavery had little intention of sharing public life with Blacks, let alone socializing with them. Little wonder, then, that in American society at large, most African-Americans' experiences did not change that much between the end of the Civil War and the ensuing decades. And by the 1890s, "Jim Crow" laws across the South took away many of the rights of African-Americans; the Supreme Court's *Plessy v. Ferguson* decision in 1896—upholding "separate but equal" facilities as constitutional --effectively confirmed that American society could remain segregated.

This was as true in the Army as anywhere else, which segregated its units by race for nearly another century. In 1866, Congress authorized the Army to have sixty seven regiments - fifty infantry, twelve cavalry, and five artillery. Of this number, four infantry and two cavalry regiments were specifically directed to be filled by black soldiers. In 1869, the number of infantry regiments was reduced from four to two.[33]

The four all-black Army regiments authorized in 1866 served with distinction on the Western frontier for the next forty years, fighting the Indian Wars and contributing much to border service. Because of their skin color and thick hair, they received the nickname of "Buffalo Soldiers" from their adversaries among the Cheyenne, Kiowa, and Apache tribes, a name that still resounds proudly across America, even in the twenty-first century.[34]

Noticeably missing from this new army, so open to Black soldiers and so aware of their contribution to the Indian wars, were Black officers from West Point. True, eventually African-Americans could rise through the ranks and gain commissions as officers. But until 1870 no African-American had even gained admission to West Point. However, one achievement of the Reconstruction governments would help to contribute to this breakthrough: the establishment of free schools for African-Americans as well as whites. It would be schooling in the South as well as the North that now opened the way to West Point; at the same time, it would be a deficiency in their education that would make graduation from West Point so challenging for these first African-American candidates. How they handled this is the story that follows.

ENDNOTES: Chapter 1

1. Stephen E. Ambrose. *Duty, Honor,. Country: A History of West Point.* (Baltimore, 1966) p,9
2. Ernest R. Dupuy, *Men of West Point. The First 150 Years of the United States Military Academy* (New York, 1951) p. 8
3. Ernest R. Dupuy. *Where They Have Trod: The West Point Tradition in American Life.* (New York, 1940) pp. 34-46
5. Theodore Crackel. Mr. Jefferson's Army (New York, 1987)
6. Ibid, pp. 54-73
7. Weigley, Russell F. *History of the United States Army.* (Bloomington IN, 1984), pp. 144-147; Ambrose, *Duty*, pp. 62-86
8. Ibid, pp146-158
9. Ibid, p. 155
10. Ambrose, *Duty*, p.128
11. Females were not admitted until 1976 and the first females graduated from West Point in 1980.
12. Henry O. Flipper. The Colored cadet at West Point. (New York, 1878) p. 18
13. Ibid
14. Ibid, p.19
15. Ibid. pp. 170-173
16. Ibid
17. Ibid
18. Ambrose, Duty, pp 106-124
19. Ibid, pp 91-194, 124

20 Samuel E. Morison, Henry S. Commager, and William E. Leuchtenberg. *The Growth of the American Republic.* (New York, 1961), pp. 548-556.
21 Ibid
22 William S. Michie. "Caste at West Point." *The North American Review.* Vol. CXXX (June 1880), p. 604.
23 Ambrose, *Duty*, pp. 112-113
24 Ibid, pp 128-30
25 Ibid, p.129
26 Ibid. pp. 170-173
27 Ibid p. 180. Dupuy, *Where They Have Trod*, p. 297
28 Ambrose, *Duty*, pp. 190-193
29 Ibid, pp. 217-219
30 James L. Morrison, Jr. "The United States Military Academy, 1833-1866: Years of Progress and Turmoil," Unpublished Ph. D.dissertation, Columbia University, 1970, p. 102
31 Ibid, pp. 102-103
32 Walter S. Dillard. "The United States Military Academy, 1865-1900: the Uncertain Years.." Unpublished Ph.D. dissertation, University of Washington, 1972, p. 93
33 Lanning, p. 64
34 William H. Leckie, *The Buffalo Soldiers* (Norman, OK,1967).

CHAPTER 2

African-Americans and Military Service

The army that African-Americans applicants to West Point hoped to serve in was, to be sure, a segregated army. But they could take some pride in knowing that African-Americans had served as individual soldiers, literally offering their lives for their country, from our earliest days as a nation. The fear of slave insurrections had kept blacks out of the ranks of local militia at first, although some did serve in the French and Indian War. But with the coming of the Revolutionary war their presence in the ranks became a political issue of interest, for now there could be no suggestion that they might be fighting as mercenaries or adventurers. Clearly, they were risking their lives to win their own freedom as well as an independent American state.

On April 19, 1775, blacks took part in the battles of Lexington and Concord, and one of the first fatalities on Lexington Green was a black soldier in Captain John Parker's company of minutemen, Price Estabrook. With war now loose in the land, the Committee of Public Safety, a revolutionary body, met in May 1775 to determine whether or not blacks could serve in the rebel cause. It decided they could, but only freemen and not slaves, for their service would be "inconsistent with the principles that are to be supported, and reflect dishonor on this Colony."[1]

This prohibition probably had little effect. Although their numbers were small, both free blacks and slaves were already under arms. In the battle of Bunker Hill on June 17, 1775, the death of Major John Pitcairn, the British commander, was widely attributed to a shot fired by Peter Salem, who had been emancipated just before the battle.[2] On the day of the Battle of Bunker

Hill, the Continental Congress took control of the colonial militia and organized the Continental Army, with George Washington as its commander. Washington, like many other Founding Fathers, was a slave owner himself, and wanted no black soldiers in his ranks, fearing they might serve as an inducement to his or any other slaves to seek their freedom through military service. His adjutant issued an order on July 7, 1775, that the Continental Army would not allow the enlistment in its ranks of "any deserter from the Ministerial [British] army, nor any stroller, Negro, or vagabond."

But hard times ensued, and after three months, Washington and his staff reopened discussions about military personnel. Once again, prejudice and property concerns carried the day, and both slaves and free blacks were forbidden to enlist. The Continental Congress backed him up, ordering that blacks should be rejected as enlistees. On November 12, 1775, Washington issued an order prohibiting the enlistment of blacks and directing that those already under arms must leave when their enlistments expired. The various colonial militia all fell in line with similar orders.[3]

Reliable communications were notoriously slow during that period, but this constituted a major opportunity for the English, whether they realized it or not, and by their actions they took advantage of it. John Murray, Earl of Dunmore and Royal Governor of Virginia, issued the following proclamation on November 7, 1775: "I do hereby...declare all endentured servants, Negroes, or others (appertaining to rebels) free, that are able and willing to bear arms, they joining His Majesty's troops, as soon as may be, for the more speedily reducing this Colony to a proper dignity."[4]

This proclamation was issued five days before Washington's formal order prohibiting blacks from the ranks of the Continental Army. When he learned of it, he and other slaveholders across Virginia were truly frightened. Just before Christmas, Washington wrote Richard Henry Lee that Dunmore would have to be soundly defeated by spring, else he would become the major threat to the rebellion. His forces would grow "as a snowball, by rolling; and faster, if some expedient cannot be hit upon to convince the slaves and servants of the impotency of his designs."[5]

By December 31, Washington had backed down and permitted the enlistment of free blacks in the Continental Army. But he retained the ban on slaves as soldiers, and the beacon of freedom still guided runaway slaves to British lines or camps. Dunmore left Virginia a few months after his proclamation, but by that time, some 700 slaves had reached his lines, and the prospect of his promise had lit fires in the hearts of thousands.[6]

For the next several years, the policies of the Continental Army and the various militia were gradually relaxed so that, by 1778, Massachusetts and Rhode Island established separate black companies. New York then offered freedom to all black slaves who would enlist for three years, and most states, by the closing days of the war, were recruiting slaves in return for freedom at the end of their enlistment. Only Georgia and South Carolina, both slave-heavy states, resisted to the bitter end, refusing to accept black soldiers in their ranks.[7]

Out of the roughly 200,000 men who fought on the rebel side during the American Revolutionary War, approximately 5,000 were black. Massachusetts fielded two all-black companies of soldiers, while Connecticut and Rhode Island contributed one each. But the vast majority of black soldiers served in completely integrated units, not only from northern states, but from southern as well. And their absorption was so complete that one Hessian soldier said: "no regiment is to be seen in which there are not Negroes in abundance: and among them are able-bodied, strong, and brave fellows."[8]

The restoration of peace meant the flourishing of slavery and the slave trade, even though many Americans were beginning to feel great unease about slavery. But the sense of racial difference had become so pervasive that many, perhaps most whites feared there was no realistic possibility that, even freed, blacks would be able to live peaceably in the same nation as whites. One of the early national leaders to articulate such feelings was Thomas Jefferson, who said it was impossible to "encorporate [sic] the blacks into the state [given the] deep-seated prejudices entertained by the whites" [9]

On May 8, 1792, Congress passed a Militia Act calling for the enrollment of "each and every able-bodied white citizen between the ages of 18 and 45," but ironically, blacks were excluded everywhere but in the deep south, where their services were still used, primarily in support roles. On July 11, 1798, Congress passed an act calling for the formal organization and establishment of a Marine Corps, and specifying that "no Negroes, Mulattoes, or Indians" could enlist. The secretary of the navy, Benjamin Stoddart, issued an order that also specified "no Negroes, Mulattoes, or Indians" could enlist. But the Navy, having to compete for labor, had less freedom than the Marines, and this rule on race was honored more in the breach. During the next several years, nearly every U.S. Navy warship, including its two leading ships, the *Constitution* and the *Constellation*, sailed with black crew members. The Marine Corps, however, excluded blacks from its ranks until World War II.[10]

When the War of 1812 started on June 12, 1812, the participation of blacks was initially resisted and limited for political reasons: Service in the military during the Revolutionary War had generally resulted in the later manumission of slaves so engaged. This impact on the system of slavery, which played an enormous economic role in a large part of the country, was an unacceptable risk to most politicians. They did their best to keep blacks out of the fight, and all American forces (save the navy) still retained their ban on blacks in uniform.

At the Battle of New Orleans, however, African-Americans probably performed their most effective service during the War of 1812. Andrew Jackson called for free blacks to fill out his forces as the British threatened to attack. He promised that those who enlisted would receive the same pay ($124.00) and bounty (160 acres of land) as white soldiers, and that, although their officers would be white, their non-commissioned officers would be drawn from their ranks. When the British finally made their main attack on January 6, 1815, more than 600 black soldiers, fully 10 percent of Jackson's force, fleshed out his ranks. Two black battalions in particular, one of some 280 men, the other 150 men, were protected by ingenious and effective breastworks of dirt and cotton bales near the center of Jackson's lines. There, they received and repelled much of the brunt of the British attack. The attackers suffered 1,500 casualties in what was the worst British defeat of the war, compared with fewer than 60 on the American side. And Jackson kept his promises of land and money to his soldiers, both black and white.[11]

But after the war, old habits returned. In 1820, the Army specified that "No Negro or mulatto will be received as a recruit of the Army." In 1821, Army regulations specified that only "free white male persons" could enlist. The Navy retained blacks as 10 percent of its force at the end of the war, but in 1839 limited black enlistments to 5 percent. It was a purely white force of 160,000 men, then, that served on the ground in the war against Mexico in 1846-48. However, some 1,000 black sailos served aboard the Navy ships that transported men and supplies or blockaded Mexican ports during that war.[12]

After Fort Sumter fell in April 1861, volunteers flooded the Union Army's recruiting officers throughout the North, and blacks were often quite eager to serve. After all, it appeared to many, slavery was the source of the fight, and so victory for the North would destroy it. In city after city, they stepped forward to serve. But all these requests for service by African-Americans were refused. Most people in the North still believed this would be a short war, and

Lincoln was primarily concerned about preserving the Union; he did not want to suddenly transform this crisis into an abolitionist crusade.

Then in the spring of 1861, a number of runaway slaves sought refuge at Fort Monroe on the Virginia Peninsula. The commander, General Benjamin Butler, refused to return them to their owners, claiming them to be "contraband of war" liable to confiscation because of the Virginia Act of Secession. Other generals spoke out in favor of returning runaways to their owners or simply did so without comment, and the government in Washington was silent for several months. Finally, on August 6, 1861, the Confiscation Act was passed that declared that any property used with the owner's consent in furtherance of the insurrection could be confiscated by the United States. Although the Act did not specify that, in the case of slaves, their confiscation meant their permanent freedom, this was its practical effect.[13]

But manpower soon became strained, and there was no conscription act in place. In 1862, some local commanders began to recruit and even impress blacks into their ranks in order to make up their requirements. On July 17, 1862, Congress authorized their recruitment while passing the antislavery Second Confiscation Act. On August 25, 1862, the War Department echoed this recruitment authorization, but limited it to 5,000 men for guard and labor duty.[14]

There remained confusion on this issue, however, until 22 September 1862, when Lincoln issued his Preliminary Emancipation Proclamation, promising that all slaves held within the Confederacy would be free on 1 January 1863. Lincoln signed the Emancipation Proclamation on New Year's Day, 1863. Therein, he said that former slaves "of suitable condition will be received into the armed service of the United States to garrison forts, positions, stations, and other places, and to man vessels of all sorts in said service."[15]

The Civil War service of African-Americans was dramatic, as they flooded to the colors. On 22 May 1863, the War Department authorized the Bureau of Colored Troops, and within a few months, there were thirty regiments of African-Americans serving as U.S. Colored Troops. Two units of African-Americans led by white officers were raised in the North as well as one in South Carolina. Their eventual numbers rose to 120 regiments of infantry, 13 of artillery, and seven of cavalry, consisting of a total of more than 186,000 men.[16]

While these men formed the 149 segregated combat regiments and labor units, thousands more also served as laborers, teamsters, and cooks. In the

Navy, however, there was no such racial segregation by ship or by organization. Around 9-10,000 blacks served in the U.S. Navy during the Civil War, some 10 percent of its wartime strength.[17]

During the Civil War, the African-American soldiers in the Union Army served almost exclusively in units known as "United States Colored Troops" led primarily by white officers. A number of these African-American soldiers, however, obtained commissions as officers, and by the end of the war, the proportion of officers to enlisted soldiers among African-Americans had risen to nearly one out of every two thousand. Most of these commissioned officers served as chaplains or as physicians or in other service roles, but they also filled infantry and artillery command posts.[18]

Although they volunteered their lives for their country, African-American soldiers found that they filled more than their proportionate share of fatigue duties, spending more time digging and carrying and fetching and burying than fighting. They were, of course, roundly despised in the Confederate states. But despite their obvious willingness to share the sacrifices inherent in war, they unfortunately were not held in very high esteem by many in the North outside abolitionist circles. More bluntly stated, newly freed slaves were strongly disparaged by most Americans, less so perhaps in the North, but even there they were considered an inferior class of humanity.[19]

In July 1863, a Union attack over open ground against several thousand Confederate soldiers holding Fort Wagner, which guarded the mouth of Charleston harbor in South Carolina, was led by the African-American soldiers of the 54th Massachusetts Regiment of Volunteers. Although they failed to take the Confederate bastion, their selfless action was at great cost (and was the focus of the 1989 award-winning movie *Glory*). They showed that they could and would fight even under the most harrowing conditions and against long odds. Their presence in Yankee uniforms might even provide the margin of difference in the Civil War.[20]

The only immediate response southerners had available took the form of threats. In May 1863, the Confederate government condemned any Union white officers who led African-American troops against their forces to the death penalty. Of course, they would have to be captured first, and it was unclear that the Confederates would carry out this threat when the opportunity presented itself. But they also threatened enslavement or re-enslavement to any African-American soldiers they might capture in a Union uniform. That threat, it was clear, would be carried out.

Some African-American soldiers and their white officers paid a great price for their service. For instance, in the battle of Fort Pillow in April 1864, troops under Nathan Bedford Forrest (himself a slave trader before the war and the first national leader of the Ku Klux Klan after it) killed about 100 African-American soldiers and several of their white officers as they were surrendering.[21]

On July 30, 1863, Lincoln had signed a retaliatory order that one Confederate officer held as a prisoner of war by the Union would be executed for each white officer executed by the Confederacy, and one Confederate prisoner would be subjected to hard labor for each captured African-American condemned to slavery.[22] After the Fort Pillow massacre, the cabinet discussed implementing retaliatory measures, but decided to do nothing unless they actually captured some of Forrest's soldiers who had been at Fort Pillow.

The U.S. Colored Troops proved a major boon to the Union cause, for even if they only freed other troops for combat, they performed an important service. Escaped slaves, who made up the great majority of the African-American troops in the U.S. Army, not only added to the Union's military strength, but they also took their labor away from the Confederacy.

After the end of the Civil War and the enactment of the Thirteenth Amendment and its implementing legislation, the civil rights of all African-Americans, whether former slaves or freedmen, were at least theoretically much the same as those of any white American. But in most circumstances, such legal provisions were generally of only limited effect. Longstanding customs and experiences were too strongly ingrained in social relations between the races to make much dramatic change in the short run possible.

This was as true in the Army as anywhere else, which segregated its units by race for nearly another century. In 1866, Congress authorized the Army to have sixty-seven regiments - fifty infantry, twelve cavalry, and five artillery. Of this number, four infantry regiments and two cavalry regiments were specifically directed to be filled by black soldiers. In 1869, the infantry regiments was reduced from four to two. [23]

The four all-black Army regiments authorized in 1866 served with distinction on the Western frontier for the next forty years, fighting the Indian Wars and contributing much to border service. From their adversaries among the Cheyenne, Kiowa, and Apache tribes, they received the nickname of "Buffalo Soldiers," a name that resounds proudly across America still, even in the twenty-first century.[24]

But the segregation of military units continued until President Harry S. Truman, by executive order, established a nondiscriminatory policy for the military in 1948, although it took several years until this order was implemented.[25] Segregation of units had not been the source of any great public concern from either side of the color line within the Army, and the various segregated black units were recognized as good fighting units with proud traditions from the Indian Wars through the Spanish American War. But in the twentieth century, being part of an all-African-American unit began to be seen as somewhat of a stigma, and in the Korean War, these units were dissolved and replaced by fully integrated units. The desired goals of cohesive, effective, and successful fighting organizations were quickly attained. Unfortunately, this was not the army in which the 19th century African-American West Pointers sought their commissions as officers.

ENDNOTES: Chapter 2

1   Michael Lanning. *The African-American Soldier*. (Secausus, N.J., 1997) pp.8-9
2   Ibid
3   Ibid, pp. 9-10
4   John H. Franklin and Alfred A. Moss Jr., *From Slavery to Freedom*,(New York, 1994), pp. 72-74.
5   Ibid, p. 74
6   Benjamin Quarles, *The Negro in the Making of America* (New York, 1964) pp. 65-66.
7   Franklin and Moss, pp 75-78.
8   Ibid, pp. 76-77
9   George M. Frederickson, *The Black Image in the White Mind*, (Princeton, NJ, 1989), p.4.
10 Lanning, pp. 16-19
11 Franklin and Moss, pp. 108-110; Lanning, pp.23-25
12 Lanning, pp. 27-29.
13 Franklin and Moss, pp. 198-200
14 Weigley, p. 211
15 Ibid, p. 212
16 Ibid. The best book on how African- Americans felt and acted during the Civil War is James McPherson's *The Negro's Civil War*. (New York, 1965, 1991)
17 Morris Macgregor. *Integration of the Armed Forces*. (Washington DC, 1989), p. 4
18 Joseph T. Glatthaar, *Forged in Battle, the Civil War Alliance of Black Soldiers and White Officers* (New York, 1990) p.82. Glatthaar lists 77 names of African-American officers who served with the Union Army in the Civil War.

19 Ibid, Chapter 10, pp 169-206, "Prejudice in the Service", and Chapter 12, pp 231-264,"Life After the USCT."
20 Lanning, pp.43-47
21 Jack Hurst, *Nathan Bedford Forrest*,(New York, 1993) pp. 165-181.
22 Roy A. Basler, ed., *Collected Works of Abraham Lincoln*, (New Brunswick, NJ, 1953), VI, p. 357
23 Lanning, p. 64
24 William H. Leckie, *The Buffalo Soldiers* (Norman,OK,1967).
25 Weigley, p. 555

This illustration from *Frank Leslie's Illustrated Newspaper* (January 12, 1871) depicts James Smith standing as he defends himself at his court martial.

CHAPTER 3

The First Black Cadets

In the days after the Civil War, "Radical Republicans" and some of their extremist political allies devoted significant political efforts to the admission of blacks into virtually all public areas of American life. There was considerable opposition to these efforts, of course, but personal feelings about how much equality with whites should be available to blacks ranged across a wide spectrum. By 1870, most Republicans felt that blacks should be allowed to vote and most Democrats felt that they should not. But that was an issue of public acceptance; on a private, social level, most white Americans of either or no party had great difficulty accepting blacks as their equals.

Between 1870 and 1900, a total of twelve African-Americans would be admitted to the Academy, but only six lasted more than one semester and only three graduated. In addition to the challenge presented by academic courses and military training, these often poorly educated young men were increasingly disadvantaged by the social ostracism shown them by all other cadets.

After the end of the Civil War, no laws or rules, military or civilian, precluded the appointment of African-Americans to West Point. But since these appointments were to be made by members of Congress, there was often a political price involved: no member insecure in his job would have appointed a black man from a district whose voting population was white, and among whom blacks were often looked down upon and even despised.

For carpetbagger Congressmen, elected to office in the South by a combination of newly-enfranchised freed slaves and "scalawags" (native

Southern whites who joined the Republicans during Reconstruction), angering the conservative white electorate was not the prohibitive problem they might have confronted elsewhere in trying to appoint a black to West Point. The real handicap to appointments of former slaves to West Point was, right after the war, a rather strict set of entrance requirements. Cadets appointed to West Point were to report by 25 May to undergo a strenuous series of entrance exams. If they passed them, they would be examined once again by the Academy's Academic Board - the superintendent and the head of each of the academic departments - the following January. Before they reported, candidates were advised in writing that they must be at least seventeen but not more than twenty-two years of age, at least five feet tall, and " free of any infectious or moral disorder, and, generally, free from any deformity, disease, or infirmity which may render them unfit for arduous military service. They must be proficient in Reading and Writing; in the elements of English Grammar; in Descriptive Geography, particularly of our own country, and in the History of the United States. In Arithmetic, the various operations in addition, subtraction, multiplication, and division, reduction, simple and compound proportion, and vulgar and decimal fractions, must be thoroughly understood and readily performed."[1]

A list of "leading physical disqualifications" followed, and it included impaired vision, unsound teeth, speech impediments, skin problems, head injuries, deafness, ulcers, hernias, and many more. In short, this would be a difficult series of hurdles for any healthy and reasonably well educated middle-class male teenager of European American extraction; for an African-American former slave, the challenge must have seemed insuperable.[2]

But this was not about to stop Congressman Benjamin F. Butler from the Fifth Congressional District of Massachusetts, a late convert to abolitionism who had used opposition to slavery as a strong political card in his home district. He became the first Congressman to consider appointing an African-American to West Point. During the Civil War, Butler was a general in the Union Army, but since he had attained that rank politically, his record as a military leader was somewhat thin. Some of his actions in uniform, however, such as his declaration that runaway slaves who came within his lines at Fort Monroe were "contraband" and would not be returned to their owners, were more political than military. After the war, it was to the political world on Capitol Hill that he returned.

In 1867, Butler sought to appoint an outstanding African-American to West Point. He fully realized that whomever he selected, as the first cadet from his race, would have to be truly exceptional. He sought the help in his search of James Fairchild, president of racially integrated Oberlin College in Ohio. But Fairchild found himself stymied: Those African-American students at Oberlin he thought intelligent enough to handle the challenge were either physically flawed or, in Fairchild's estimation, would be unable to handle the non-academic pressures, including insult; those who could handle the social pressures and physical challenges were not thought to have sufficient intellectual ability. Butler was deeply disappointed by this initial failure, but he persevered.[3]

In 1870, three years after Butler's first failure to find an acceptable candidate, he came upon a young man he thought good enough to stand up to the challenges that awaited him at West Point. The first African-American actually named to the secretary of war in a request for an appointment to West Point was Charles Sumner Wilson, nominated by Butler on March 7, 1870. [4].

But Butler's efforts, however genuine, were again frustrated in this instance. Many cadets had been admitted to West Point before the Civil War at ages younger than 17 (including George McClellan, the "Young Napoleon" who had entered West Point in 1842 at the age of fifteen, ranked second academically in his class at graduation, and twice commanded the Union army in the early days of the Civil War). But in 1866, Congress had passed a joint resolution that incoming cadets at West Point must be between the ages of 17 and 22, except for certain Civil War veterans. Wilson was only 16 years old and he would not be 17 years of age on 1 July 1870, the day on which, should he pass the rigorous entrance examinations, he would be sworn in as a Cadet. He was not appointed to West Point.[5]

However, two more blacks were nominated to enter West Point in 1870. In April, Michael Howard was nominated by Congressman Legrand W.Perce of Mississippi, and in May, James Webster Smith was nominated by Congressman S.L.Hoge of South Carolina. [6]. Both reported to West Point on May 24, where they would take the required admissions tests toward the end of June. Until that time, they were kept busy with training in rudimentary military skills such as marching and reporting.

Howard was the first to catch popular attention. *The New York Sun* on May 25, 1870, carried a story about him that gives considerable insight into the circumstances confronting newly arrived black appointees seeking admission to West Point. The very headline of the article, although intended to be sarcastic—"The West Point Revels"—gives some sense of contemporaneous attitudes widely shared by white people, both at West Point and, for that matter, across the entire country. For these people, the arrival of black candidates for admission to West Point represented a major disruption in the way things had long been. And despite the high-minded attitude toward the social progress of black Americans displayed by the author of the article, for most white Americans, the disruption is what mattered.

The article signaled its point of view with its subhead, "The Condemnation of the Caucasian Snobs…A Plot to Trip Him in his Examination," and in its opening paragraph: "West Point and the whole National Academy were almost breathless with excitement yesterday. The son of an American colored citizen arrived here in his new role of military cadet. There had been rumors that negro boys had been appointed to the National Academy, but the absolute arrival of an African, commission in hand, is too much for West Point human nature to endure. Aristocratic professors and jaunty cadets are speechless. The time for the breaking forth of their indignation has not yet arrived. They cannot do the subject justice, but their indignant countenances and ominous looks indicate the coming storm."

The article continued: "Young Howard is a full black of sturdy physique…. and is as bright a boy as was ever seen. His hair is cut tight, and his accent smacks decidedly of the plantation….It is settled that he cannot be rejected physically by the Medical Board….The white cadets seemed paralyzed. "It is dreadful" says one. "Let's put the nigger in the river" says another. Some of them threaten to resign, while others talk of killing the black boy outright. One young Democrat from Illinois exclaimed: "Great God, what shall we do? He will have to drill with us for four weeks before the examination anyway. He will have to be bilged."

The correspondent then concluded with what seems to be, however unsettling, a fair and prescient summation: "One thing is certain, the black cadet is here. He is undoubtedly physically qualified. He must now drill with the white cadets until the examination on 24 July. Then he will fail in mental examination, and go back to Mississippi. This is the programme, for the examining officers have power to reject any applicant…. But in the light of the Fifteenth Amendment, what shall we do with the African in our National and Naval Academies is a grave question for the unregenerate mind."[7]

The attitudes here attributed to cadets are in keeping with those commonly held by many whites across the country in 1870. Thus, although the cadets whose comments are reported in the article remain anonymous, there seems little doubt that young men around the age of twenty probably did make them. The Civil War had awakened many white Americans to the basic humanity of blacks, all of whom were now free. Ardent abolitionists, the "Radical Republicans," had firm control of the national government. But change comes slowly, and most white Americans still considered blacks an inferior race. Admission of a black to West Point, no matter the specific qualifications of a particular nominee, was simply going too far, too fast, for probably the great majority of white Americans. That some of these young men, appointed to West Point from varied social settings across the land, still accepted the deep-set and long-standing prejudices of their families and friends should not be a surprise.

No doubt the other cadet candidates who were showing up at the same time were free with commentary - such is the stuff of youth. But the reporter was not terribly careful with some of his details. For one, citing no evidence he claimed that there was to be a plot by the officers to fail Howard in the academic exams. True, Howard failed in each of the six areas in which he was tested (Arithmetic, Reading, Writing, Grammar, Geography, and History), and even failure in one of these areas was enough for other candidates to be refused admission. However, Howard was only one among 48 cadet candidates who failed the academic admission tests. Four cadet candidates were rejected medically, and, for a variety of other reasons that included the death of one nominee, 13 failed to report. Only 38 cadet candidates nominated for appointment to West Point in the summer of 1870 passed the rigorous academic tests and were admitted, and among their number was the other black candidate, James Webster Smith, who had no problem passing his examinations. [8]

There is no proof that Michael Howard was refused admission simply because he was black and some other New York newspapers were not so hard on the officers and cadets at West Point. On 10 June, the *New York Tribune* told its readers "why the colored candidates for cadetship were rejected": "When young Howard reached West Point, it could readily be discovered that he had received little or no education. He said he had not been educated, that he had not been at school over a year.... When his mental or scholastic test took place, it was almost a total failure, and he was pronounced against by the Examining Board, and therefore cannot enter as a cadet." The article then went on to explain why James W. Smith was also rejected: Smith "has a nervous affection of the eyes, and goes nearly blind at times. He also has an affection of the lungs, and it is well known that he is generally in bad health. He is, however, very intelligent, having gone through a course of studies at the Howard University, and would probably pass the mental and scholastic examination, but the law of Congress prevents his admission on account of the physical disability."

Having provided this apparently objective explanation, the article then proceeded to another level of justification: "These two colored boys have been treated with uniform kindness at the Academy, and the tricks that the boys usually play on new comers have been omitted in their cases, because the cadets thought the people would say they were roughly handled because they were colored boys. They eat at the same table with the others, and have been subject to the same rules, and under the same protection."[9]

It is interesting to note that this article appeared two weeks before the entrance exams began, and wrongly stated that both Howard and Smith had been denied admission, which, as we have seen, was only true for Howard. Unlike the earlier *Sun* article, which was written by a reporter on the scene, this one was constructed from information released by an official U.S. Army source in Washington, D.C., which perhaps explains why it says that such favorable treatment was accorded black cadets.

On that same 10 June 1870, the *New York Times* also ran an article on black cadets that asserted: "Never before in the history of this military post and college has there been so many incorrect, if not absolutely false, reports of its affairs circulated. This has been especially true of the examination exercises and in relation to the colored applicants for cadetship acceptance. The statement that they have been ill-treated in any way by the cadets is a round falsehood. The plain truth is that they have been placed upon the same formal footing as the other cadets. That there has been a great deal of feeling among many officers, cadets and civilians concerning the presence and disposition of these new "amendments" is true. But this feeling has been more of perplexity and anxiety than anything else in the effort to divine the policy that should prevail, and to mark the line between the social and the official treatment."

The *Times* article, however, did concede the following: "The nearest approach to real trouble has been in the Mess Department. At first, it was debated whether the colored ones should have a separate table and waiter. Col Black decided that the cadets should be 'free and equal,' and that neither white nor black distinction should be made. The white waiters, who manifested some signs of dissatisfaction, were assembled in the presence of the officers and informed that unless they were willing to serve all the guests of the table alike, they must withdraw. They have remained. So the colored cadets eat side by side with their paler comrades. They also room in the barracks the same as the others, and they are saluted and attended to, in all their inquiries and duties, just as though their skins had been bleached before they entered the Academy."[10]

Clearly, the three newspapers quoted above got some of the facts wrong and perhaps exaggerated some others to make particular points, but that is to be expected. Other New York newspapers gave the story no more than a few lines, or even ignored it completely: Between 15 May and 30 June, 1870, for example, the *New York World* ran articles about West Point on 4, 9, and 11 June but they dealt with graduation and other issues and did not mention black cadets once.

What sort of role, then, did the New York newspapers play in this controversy? Since black cadets came from homes across the country, the papers could not have been involved in the politics of individual appointments. But they often had long-established political standards to uphold, and the more abolitionist papers would have been expected to play up the side of the oppressed black. As will be seen in the case of Cadet James Smith, individual supporters of black cadets were not above betraying their confidences and conveying "inside stories" of their plights to New York newspapers, with the apparent idea that public shame would cause the authorities at West Point to amend the racist ways of their white cadets. And there seems to have been an unofficial network of some sort that conveyed to New York newspapers the anticipated arrival of black cadet candidates at West Point, which would explain why reporters were there waiting for what they would have seen as a potentially compelling story. As was mentioned in the introduction, in the nineteenth century there was no formal way in which West Point authorities would have routinely learned that a black cadet candidate had been nominated before his arrival. While there may have been some unofficial means of communication that might have alerted them, it could easily have been the case that newspapers knew more about the anticipated arrival of blacks than did the authorities at West Point.

New York newspapers put different emphasis on the political issues surrounding black West Point cadets. Seen from a purely commercial perspective, they were basically competing for the same readers, and so would have been expected to report that which they thought was important to the general public, that which would sell newspapers. If we look beyond the established political stance of a given newspaper, then, the differing focus of various publications is perhaps understandable in this way--as differing assessments of the marketplace for these stories. There were certainly cases when some New York newspapers put flesh on the bones by publicizing events that otherwise would have disappeared, issues that would have been protected as internal to West Point and thus passed unnoticed by a wider public. But the approaches taken by different New York newspapers indicate by their variety that there was no uniformly settled or even widely accepted position on this sudden access to favored positions by young men who were black and often former slaves.

In the nineteenth century, admission statistics varied widely, but the lack of racial bias shown toward Howard's nomination seems clear. This is shown in the light of statistics from the following year, 1871, when 60 cadet candidates passed the academic admissions tests and were admitted. Only 22 failed the academic admissions tests in 1871, while 10 were rejected by the Medical Board and another 11 simply failed to report. And among the 60 nominees who were admitted to West Point in 1871 was Henry Alonzo Napier, a black from Tennessee. All of which is not to say that there was no anti-black race prejudice openly evidenced by cadets and others at West Point. Quite to the contrary, there was indeed, and it lasted, tolerated even in its overt form by the official Army command at West Point, until well after World War II. The overt exclusion of black cadets from the private lives shared by white cadets in their off-duty hours is the most dramatic statement of prejudice that endured at West Point.

Perhaps looking at a particular incident in the early days of Howard and Smith at West Point provides some insight into the massive and all-pervasive nature of the prejudice they faced. While they were awaiting their admission tests toward the end of June, the cadet candidates lived in tents and were given rudimentary military training. On occasion, one of their number would be temporarily appointed to direct the movement of a group of these cadet candidates. On June 6, just such a one, a Mister McChord from Kentucky, was told to march a group of cadet candidates or "New Cadets" (which group included the two blacks, Howard and Smith) over to the shoeblack's place, that they might all have their shoes blackened. Upon arrival at the shoeblack's, the white cadets went in first, and left the two black cadets outside. McChord explicitly ordered that the blacks were to have their shoes blackened last, after all the white cadets had been serviced. A certain amount of unpleasantness then occurred.

Some might describe the events as little more than a tempest in a teapot, as, indeed, the officers in charge at West Point ultimately did. But to capture the full flavor of the affair, complete with a sense of the innate bias against blacks harbored by many (if not most) whites at the time, the events are best related in the words of the participants and the official investigation that followed. The first report was submitted by Michael Howard and stated: "While I was waiting at the door for the others to have their boots blacked so that I could get in, the cadet who marched the squad over there stepped up to me and, striking me in the face, said: 'get away from this door.' Mr. Smith, who was standing near, asked him what right he had to strike anyone. He said he was an officer. Mr. Smith said officers don't strike their soldiers. The Cadet put his hand in his pocket for his knife and said he would cut Mr. Smith open. Thereupon nearly the whole squad began to yell, 'kill the d-d nigger; cut him open; knock him down, &c.' But some of them told him to let us alone, and he went back in the room. But when I went in soon after, and got upon the bench, he borrowed a knife from one of the other Cadets, and holding it open in his right hand he grasped my coat collar with his left hand and jerked me down from the bench."[11]

New Cadet McChord submitted his report in which he claimed that "each man, as soon as his shoes were blacked, took his place out under the stoop to await the others; but in the meantime, the colored cadets took their position against the facing on each side of the door, and blocked it up so completely that it was with difficulty that the other members of the squad could pass out. I went up to the one who was obstructing the way mostly, and requested him three times in a gentlemanly manner, to stand on the other side, which he failed to do. I then upon the impulse of the moment struck him on the side of the face, but would not have done so had I reflected a moment."[12]

Further evidence gathered by the investigating officer, Captain Alexander S. Clarke, commandant of the new cadets, from Mr. McChord extended his above written statement. He did not mention pulling Howard off the bench with one hand, a knife held in the other in an obviously threatening manner. Instead McChord claimed: "The third time, I struck him on the side of the face. I went out under the stoop where the other cadets were, and borrowed a knife from one of my classmates, and remained out there about ten minutes, with the knife still in my hand. I then went in and got on the bench, so that I could have my shoes blacked after the one in front of me had his, and started to put my foot on the block, when Cadet Howard jumped on the bench, and I pushed him off with my elbow. I did not borrow the knife for the purpose of cutting him or anyone, but had it for some purpose while under the porch, and still kept it in my hand, working the blade with my thumb.[13]

The final report, a summary of formal reports by the New Cadets involved, was submitted by Captain Clarke, to Colonel H.M. Black, the Commandant of Cadets, and concluded: "From all accounts, it is evident that these colored cadets took their positions in or near the doorway, so that to pass them, the white ones were obliged to rub against them, and that Mr. Howard refused to move when ordered to do so by Mr. McChord, who was in command of the squad. Mr. McChord undoubtedly struck Mr. Howard, but was no doubt angered by the manner of Mr. H. I have not been able to get the same account of the affair from Mr. Howard twice, but each time differs from the others, and from these discrepancies and the difference between his statements and that of New Cadet Smith (also colored), I am of the opinion that both of these youths have greatly exaggerated an insignificant affair and that they have agreed between themselves so to do.... I think Mr. H.'s punishment is the inevitable result of his attempting to push himself in the way of his white comrades.... and while I do not attempt to uphold Mr. McChord, [I] think the mitigating circumstances such as to require no further action taken in the matter, except a private reprimand from yourself to Mr. McC."[14]

This event can give the reader, more than a century later, some sense of what we would today call the innate racism that permeated all of American white society, North as well as South. This is all the more important to note because the events occurred at West Point, the academic seat of the U.S. Army where the principal officers who fought and won the Civil War had been educated, some of whom had stayed in uniform and at the time of these events filled senior positions of leadership in the army (in 1870, those West Pointers who had fought for the South and, effectively, for the preservation of slavery, were no longer in the U.S. Army and could have no effect on the training of cadets at West Point). The point is that, if such racism occurred there, where the student body was literally drawn from around the country, and the staff and faculty was made up of active duty officers in the U.S. Army whose actions were constantly constrained by Federal laws and regulations, then it no doubt occurred in equal or stronger measure in the private sector throughout the nation. These Army officers were no doubt much more aware of the impact on their duties of the recently enacted Thirteenth and Fourteenth Amendments to the Constitution, which eliminated slavery and sought to guarantee the elevation of blacks, as far as the custodians of West Point were concerned, to the full rights of U.S. citizenship enjoyed by whites.

Thus, in his final report, Captain Clarke was careful to claim that "The same thing would doubtless have occurred had any white boy who was unpopular with his class have put himself in the same position." But would it? First of all, these "New Cadets" had been at West Point less than two weeks, and could barely have known each other, let alone the rudiments of the military. Given the widespread hostility of whites at the time to the rapid rise of blacks to prestigious stations formerly filled exclusively by whites, there would naturally have been a certain amount of personal opposition, even if subconscious, within the cadre at West Point to the sudden appearance there of potential black cadets. These young black men faced a perilous journey as they tried to break the color line at West Point.

Thus, though Clarke tried to pretend that Howard and Smith were being treated as any other white cadet could expect to be treated, it is obvious on the face of it that this is not the case. First of all, when the New Cadets were marched down to the shoeblack's place, the blacks were told they had to wait until all the whites were through before they could be served. Second, the fact that they may have stood in the doorway in a manner that would have required a white cadet going through the doorway to brush against them could not have been used to justify striking a white boy in the face with a fist. But at the time, such violent treatment was commonly accorded to blacks who dared to obstruct a white, in the North as well as in the South. And third, whichever of the two stories is more accurate - whether Howard was pulled down off the bench by McChord who then took his place, as Howard says, or was pushed off by McChord with his elbow as Howard attempted to climb up on the bench, as McChord says - is largely irrelevant. In both stories, McChord had an open knife in his right hand, and although he denied he borrowed it to threaten or cut Howard or anyone else, why did he have it in his right hand, the blade open, when he used physical force with his left hand to force Howard off the bench? Could this gesture have been anything other than a naked threat by McChord to strike Howard with a deadly weapon? If this clash had occurred between two white cadets, of course, it would have been considered a serious matter. But since this was only five years after the end of the Civil War and the emancipation of slaves throughout the land, we can see here the ways in which blacks, even in the most prestigious U.S. Army post in bedrock Yankee land fifty miles north of New York City, were without thought automatically relegated to a sort of second-class citizenship by the large majority of whites.

Howard wrote to Mississippi Senator Adelbert Ames, who forwarded his letter to the Secretary of War with a personal plea for assistance, but nothing more came of it.[15] In any case, when these cadet candidates took the admissions test, beginning on 24 June, Howard failed in all six subject areas, while Smith passed and was admitted. McChord, it is interesting to note, passed only the test in Geography, while failing in the other five tested areas, and therefore, like Howard, was refused admittance to West Point.[16] So in the summer of 1870, the only black admitted to West Point was Smith.

The son of Israel Smith, a well-to-do black carpenter, James Webster Smith was educated in a Freedmen's Bureau school in Columbia, South Carolina, before he was brought to Hartford, Connecticut by David Clark, a philanthropist who both supported and educated him. After high school graduation, he enrolled at the newly-opened Howard University in Washington, DC, but after only a few weeks there he learned that he had been given the appointment to West Point from his home district in Columbia, South Carolina.[17] When Smith arrived at West Point, he joined Michael Howard from Mississippi. As noted, there was considerable confusion among the authorities at West Point about what should be done with these first New Cadets of their race. Academy officials pretended to ignore their race, although clearly it was no accident that they were assigned to be roommates. But a *New York Sun* article of 30 June 1870 reported that many of their white colleagues were quite distressed: "Smith says that the officers and professors are very kind to him, and the older cadets never molest him, but that the members of his own class call him opprobrious names, even at table. They throw water on his and Howard's heads as they pass under the windows, and on last Monday night, they threw a pail of slops over them while they were asleep, deluging the bed with filthy water."[18]

A New Orleans newspaper ran an editorial piece on their arrival that gives an interesting insight into attitudes at the time in the most cosmopolitan city of the south. It put a twist different from that of the New York papers: "The introduction of the colored element into the classic halls of West Point has produced quite a commotion. For the credit of those colored cadets, it is well to say that, while they passed all the examinations, [the paper was in error here] forty-seven white boys were rejected. It is said that these boys will destroy the romance of the place. The ladies are indignant because their brothers and relations will have to drill as well as to mess with these newcomers...What will be the upshot of the matter is hard to tell. The negro is there, and is on an equality, in all respects, with the white cadets....Perhaps unkind treatment... may cause them to leave; but as the colored folks are good enough for us in the estimation of our northern friends, we cannot perceive why they are not good enough for them. The only serious opposition to the negro comes from those who were most zealous in the adoption of the fifteenth amendment. The blacks will soon learn that their true friends and well-wishers are the so-called rebels." [19]

This was written, of course, at a time when Reconstruction had struck hard, removing the vote of Confederate veterans while enfranchising newly freed slaves and allowing many carpetbaggers and "scalawags" to rise to positions of political power. And while some interesting points are made, the claims of true friendship for blacks on the part of "so-called rebels" must be taken with a grain of salt. And as noted, the *Picayune* got Howard's status wrong: He did not pass the entrance exams, and within a few weeks, he was gone, leaving Smith alone, the only African-American surrounded by 230 European American cadets. Although he was not particularly dark-skinned and so was not as different from other cadets as Howard had been,[20] Smith was immediately known to be a member of a race different from that of all other cadets. From the beginning, he was treated cautiously by other cadets, and by some as an automatic inferior for that reason alone. Smith was a quite intelligent youth, with considerable self-confidence and a strongly favorable appreciation of his own skills and abilities relative to those of other cadets. He was unwilling from the start to passively accept the disparagement of his peers. But his efforts to this end were not well received, and he quickly found himself ostracized, or perhaps more accurately, shunned.[21]

Thereafter, no cadets would talk to him at all other than in the course of official business (which included recitation in class). This was to become the standard treatment of all African-American cadets by their white American fellows until after World War II, though it was less strictly upheld in some cases. This ostracism was later tolerated by the authorities at West Point with the same justification that was the basis for the Army's formal racial segregation until the Korean War. A 1925 Army War College study entitled "The Use of Negro Manpower in War," had concluded that the intelligence of African-Americans was lower than that of white Americans, that they lacked courage, were superstitious, and suffered moral and character weakness. It said the "social inequality" of African-Americans made their close association with white Americans "inimical to harmony and efficiency," and became the linchpin for official Army racial discrimination.[22]

After Howard's departure, seats were assigned in the mess hall. Smith soon got into a fight for allegedly having served himself food before the other cadets at his table. This would have been an egregious breach of tradition for new cadets and the deference they were supposed to show to upperclassmen, but there may have been more to the incident, as Smith claimed. A number of cadets assigned to his table requested reassignment to another table, and because of the racial issue, what might otherwise have been little more than the harassment of a new cadet by upperclassmen grew into a considerable incident.[23]

Since his arrival, Smith had been sending letters each week to David Clark, his friend and benefactor in Hartford. When he described the mistreatment he was enduring in a letter of June 29, Clark was incensed. He took the letter to the *Hartford Courant,* which published it on July 2, and it was reprinted by many newspapers across the country: "Dear Friend," Smith's letter opened, and went on to describe the treatment he was experiencing: "And now these fellows appear to be trying to run me off, and I fear they will succeed if they continue as they have begun. We went into camp yesterday, and not a moment has passed since then but some one of them has been cursing and abusing me. All night they were around my tent, cursing and swearing at me so that I did not sleep two hours all night. It is just the same at the table, and what I get to eat I must snatch for like a dog. I don't wish to resign if I can get along at all; but I don't think it will be best for me to stay and take all the abuses and insults that are heaped upon me."

But it was not just in the off-duty routines that Smith was exposed to this kind of harassment. "One of the cadets refused to drill the squad because I was in it, and they reduced him from a corporal to a private for disobedience of orders, and they are all mad about that. The one who drills the squad now is the meanest specimen of humanity I ever saw. After marching us out to the drill ground this morning, he said to me 'Stand off one side from the line, you d----d black son of a b---h. You are too near that white man. I want you to remember that you are not on an equal footing with the white men in your class, and what you learn here you will have to pick up, for I won't teach you a d----d thing.' And thus he kept me standing until the captain came around inspecting, when he pretended that he put me there to teach me a movement which I had never practised [sic] before....If I complain of their conduct to the commandant I must prove the charge, or nothing can be done; and where am I to find one from so many to testify in my behalf?"[24]

General Oliver O. Howard, commissioner of the Freedmen's Bureau, founder and president of the new university dedicated to the education of freed men and women in Washington D.C. that bore his name, and a long-standing ally of African-Americans, encouraged Smith to withstand the insults. He also wrote to the *New York Tribune*: "Sir: I have written a short letter to Cadet Smith (the colored cadet), and the thought occurs to me that I might perhaps influence high-minded cadets in his favor by giving my letter to you for publication...If West Point has not power enough to protect such a young man as Cadet Smith - quick, able, honest, noble-spirited as he is - then West Point will have a hard struggle against the returning tide of feeling that will break in from the people. I am a graduate of West Point, and am proud of her sons who have been true to the country and true to humanity, but I am greatly ashamed when cadets dishonor us by a mean prejudice that ought long ago to have been smothered."

Howard's letter to Smith was then printed: " My Dear Young Friend: ...I do hope you will never think of giving up while you have health to stand the storm. I suffered quite as much when I first went to West Point. Endure the insults without any show of fear. A prompt and able reply when off duty will sometimes avail you. A pleasant smile will win hearts to you. God, who allowed you to be born and live with the blood of the African in your veins, will bear you through every trial. To be a soldier one need not only be brave in battle, but have an abundance of genuine fortitude, so as to bear up in disaster and apparent defeat. There is no real defeat to the true soldier - his soul is unconquerable."[25]

General Howard's heart was obviously in the right place, and his letter to Smith was well meant. But just as obviously, he had not "suffered quite as much" as Smith when he first went to West Point: He was not the only cadet of a race whose members had long occupied the lowest rungs in society, a race considered by most white Americans to be of a lower order, a race never before seriously considered eligible for cadetship at this national institution. It is true, however, that, as a cadet during the 1850s, Howard had been ostracized by all other cadets because, among other things, his peers considered him an abolitionist. And the social ostracism practiced at West Point during the nineteenth century could be brutal. The strong moral codes of the time, coupled with the closed and isolated world in which cadets lived, resulted in a social system where the acceptance by one's peers often meant everything. If a cadet was deemed by other cadets to be cowardly, ungentlemanly, or the proponent of ideas unpopular within the Corps of Cadets, he might find himself "cut": no other cadet, thereafter, would have anything to do with him outside of official business.[26]

This had happened to many cadets before African-Americans arrived at West Point, including Emory Upton, the Commandant of Cadets in Smith's day. Upton had been "cut" after he announced, just before the Civil War, that he was an abolitionist. After years of ostracism, both Howard and Upton had been able to end this state by actually fighting other cadets who had insulted them, thus apparently showing the Corps of Cadets that they really were "men" and worthy of being reaccepted into the fold.[27] But for Smith, as we shall see, such a violent reaction on his part could only have negative consequences.

Howard did have grounds, then, for claiming to have been through similar experiences of feeling desperately alone at West Point. But unlike new cadet Howard before him, new cadet Smith now found himself adrift in, and at the mercy of, a largely hostile sea of cadets of the other, traditionally superior, race. Smith found himself in a previously unknown predicament, one that was, to a white American, really quite unknowable. But Howard was outraged by Smith's plight, and he sought to publicize his concerns.

He was not alone. In Congress, Charles Sumner and Benjamin F. Butler sponsored a Resolution recommending formal investigation of Cadet Smith's experiences. The Resolution passed, but Congress elected to wait rather than press for the investigation.[28] Things were getting out of hand, and it was time for authorities at West Point to step in.

When President James Madison tried to stabilize the Military Academy in 1815, he had specified that it would have a nearly independent existence, with only the inspector of the academy - at the time, General Joseph G. Swift, the Chief of Engineers - standing in the chain of command between the superintendent and the secretary of war.[29] In Smith's time, the inspector of the academy was Major General Edmund Schriver, and in a letter to Schriver of July 11, 1870, the academy's Superintendent, Colonel Thomas G. Pitcher, elaborated on these and other issues. He had ordered Cadet Smith to report to him, verified that he had indeed written the letter to Clark, and informed him he was liable to serious charges for writing such a letter for publication. Smith assured him it was not written for publication, but was only a letter to a friend, an explanation that Pitcher accepted.

As to the language used at drill, Pitcher interrogated the accused drill master, Cadet Quincy Gillmore, and the other members of the squad, who denied the accusation or any abusive treatment of Smith. Pitcher was inclined to believe the European American cadets' version of the story. Then he discussed the situation at meals: "In the Messhall, in the reorganization of the tables, there was considerable feeling exhibited by those to whose lot it fell to have Cadet Smith at their table. The Commandant of the table, a Cadet Lieutenant, is now in arrest for neglect of duty (not sitting at his table), while others have applied to be assigned to other tables. Their request, however, was refused, and they informed that their reasons for wishing such a change could not be entertained for a moment.[30]

But the superintendent then backed away from this suggestion that he was not going to tolerate any discrimination against Smith by other cadets: "I think it highly probable that all the amenities of polite society were not observed toward him for the first few days, but I am assured by Cadets that the feeling toward the young man is improving in the Corps, and he, himself, informed me on Saturday the 9th inst. that he had no complaints to make.[31] Colonel Pitcher offered no final judgment on who was right and who was wrong, but rather proposed that, given the national publicity the case was generating, a formal court of inquiry be ordered to investigate the matter.[32] While Pitcher may not have shown a wholehearted commitment to Cadet Smith's welfare, it may well be that Pitcher did the best he could for Smith while trying to keep tension down and maintain what he saw, in context, as his responsibilities toward other cadets.

An excerpt from a letter by another cadet, James Fornance from Pennsylvania, on July 17, 1870 gives some insight into at least his feelings on this matter: "Dear Brother - ...A committee has been appointed to meet here tomorrow to investigate the negro case he is a dirty spotted nigger no one speaks to him nor has anything more to do with him than possible two cadet officers have been reduced to ranks on his account one refused to drill him and the other refused to sit at the table with him he has not washed since he reported (about the 25 of May).[33]

The court of inquiry, consisting of two generals and two majors, heard testimony at West Point. Colonel Emory Upton, commandant of cadets, testified that he had counseled one of Smith's worst antagonists. He had also lectured the entire corps of cadets on the issue, reminding them that "federal laws entitled Smith to precisely the same rights and privileges as all other cadets, and that the law should be strictly enforced." [34]

The court of inquiry found that Smith had exaggerated and that most of his charges were unfounded. The court found the authorities at West Point had treated Smith with "scrupulous fairness," and recommended that Smith be tried by a general court martial. Secretary of War Belknap stepped in on 10 August and ordered Pitcher simply to give Smith a severe reprimand.[35]

Later in August, Smith got into a fight with Cadet John Wilson, one of his classmates, over drawing water from a tank. Smith struck Wilson with his dipper, gashing his temple. A few days later, he was reported for making a disrespectful reply in ranks, which he denied in writing. But the cadet who charged him was backed up by three witnesses, and Commandant Upton filed charges against Smith for making a false statement. Secretary of War Belknap quickly ordered a General Court Martial to sit in judgment on the two charged offenses. While such a formal judicial proceeding would be most unusual at West Point today, it was not an uncommon event for cadets after the Civil War.[36]

Eight high ranking officers sat on the court, with General Howard acting as the President. After all testimony had been heard from all parties, the Court found Smith guilty of creating a disturbance at the water tank, but innocent of making a false statement. The punishment meted out was extra tours of guard duty, but for complex technical reasons that apparently involved public relations, the punishment was never exacted.

Given the tight fusion of popular attitudes among cadets, particularly on issues that affected them directly, as Smith's presence at West Point did, it would seem not unfair to surmise that most other cadets were probably quite unhappy with Smith's presence in their midst. More evidence can be found in personal memoranda of Major General Eben Swift, USMA class of 1876, who reported the words to a number of songs written and sung by cadets. A song written by Cadet Carter Howland is followed by this: "But his famous and most popular was composed by himself and was entitled 'Nigger Jim.' It was aimed at Jim Smith, the colored cadet, a repulsive looking, freckle-faced negro, who had probably been appointed by an enemy of the Academy as a living caricature upon its lofty ideals and standards. Howland blacked his face, except the part which reached from mouth to ear on each side, making it appear to be all mouth. He had a broom which he handled like a banjo and sang, to the tune of 'Little Sam':

> I'm de noted cullod ca-det and from Dixieland I came
> Where I used to hoe de cotton and de cane, all day, All de day! (Basso Profundo)
> Old Sary's doin' it for you now, dis nigger he has found
> And you won't see any more of dis, you chile Dis you chile.
> But I'll write a book on West Point and for Congress run
> And I'll engineer a bill to hang old Lyle God-damned old Lyle [37]

In December, once again Smith attracted headlines. As he walked guard, he was harassed by a number of other cadets. He warned one to stop stepping on his toes,[38] others to stop insulting him. One cadet put Smith on report, and Smith defended himself by charging his tormenters with interfering with his performance of duty. Once again, the reporting cadet said one thing, Smith another, and suddenly he was facing another court martial, this time for telling falsehoods and conduct unbecoming a gentleman. He was found guilty and sentenced to dismissal from the Academy. But newspaper headlines screamed, and the Grant administration, sensitive to the African-American vote in the South, gave Smith one more chance. Secretary Belknap, on 13 June, voided the court's decision and allowed Smith to stay at West Point, but required him to repeat his Fourth Class year.[39]

After that first year of constant crisis and turmoil, Smith stayed out of trouble. He was not court-martialed again, but he had angered many European American cadets during his first year, and their anger endured. His second year was made somewhat easier when he was joined in the summer of 1871 by another African-American, Henry Alonzo Napier from Tennessee. For a year, Smith had a roommate and a friend, which made his life much easier. But in June 1872, Napier failed math and French and left Smith once again alone. He had to wait only a month, however, when Thomas Van Rensselaer Gibbs, an African-American appointed to West Point from Florida, joined him. Gibbs lasted only until January 1873, when he, too, failed math and left the Academy. It was a full six months before Smith was joined by Henry O. Flipper from Georgia in July 1873, the fourth African-American admitted to West Point. He would be the first to graduate.[40]

ENDNOTES Chapter 3

1. Henry O. Flipper, *The Colored Cadet at West Point* (New York,1878), pp 20-21.
2. Ibid
3. Ambrose, pp. 231-232
4. Nomination form and accompanying letter from Congressman Butler to Secretary of War, dated March 7, 1870; Microfilm Collection M1002, "Selected Documents Relating to Blacks Nominated for Appointment to the U.S. Military Academy During the Nineteenth Century, 1870-1887," U.S. Archives (Hereafter referred to as "Sel. Docs.) Roll 1, pp. 31-32.
5. Sel. Docs., Roll 1, p. 37.
6. Sel. Docs., Roll 1, pp. 43-49
7. *New York Sun*, 25 May 1870.

8 Sel. Docs., Roll 1, pp. 68-72
9 *New York Tribune*, 10 June 1870.
10 *The New York Times*, 10 June 1870
11 Sel. Docs., Roll 1, p,147
12 Ibid, p.149.
13 Ibid p. 156
14
15 Howard's letter to Senator Ames is found at Ibid, p. 153; Senator Ames' note to the Secretary of War is at Ibid, p.154.
16 Ibid, p. 162
17 William P. Vaughn,"West Point and the First Negro Cadet", *Military Affairs*, Vol.XXXV, No.3, October. 1971, pp.100-102
18 *New York Sun*, June 30, 1870.
19 *New Orleans Picayune*, 9 July 1870
20 Ibid, "Smith is described as tall, slender, and rather loosely put together. He looks more like a Mongolian than an African. His eyes are almond-shaped and his forehead of the Chinese pattern. His complexion is that of an octoroon and his hair nearly straight. Howard is dark and more like the African type."
21 Ambrose, p.232. Smith's grades can be found in the U.S. Military Academy Archives, and they show that in June, 1871, after his first academic year, he was ranked 30th in Math and 20th in French out of a class of 55. He received no overall ranking because he was forced to repeat the year for disciplinary reasons. In June 1872, however, he ranked 15th out of 66 members of his class in the Order of General Merit.
22 Benjamin O. Davis Jr., *American, An Autobiography*, (Washington, DC, 1991), p.25
23 Vaughn, p. 100
24 *New York Tribune*, July 7, 1870
25 *New York Tribune,* July 12, 1870 (emphasis in original)
26 John F. Marszalek, *Assault at West Point* (New York,1994), p.16.
27 Ibid
28 Vaughn, p.101
29 Ambrose, p. 44
30 This original longhand letter, of which I was able to secure a photocopy, is preserved in the Archives of the United States Military Academy at West Point.
31 Ibid
32 Ibid
33 Letter written by Cadet James Fornance, USMA class of
1871, preserved in the Archives, U.S. Military Academy, West Point.
34 Vaughn, p.100
35 Ibid, p. 101

36 Ibid
37 Memoranda retained in Archives, U. S. Military Academy, West Point
38 At West Point, stepping on a cadet's toes imparts far more than physical pain: the toes on a cadet's shoes or boots are always spit shined to a glassy finish before he leaves his room, and if someone steps on them, that act destroys the carefully prepared shell of high gloss. Restoration consumes an hour or more of industry with a rag, water, and shoe polish by the owner of the shoes. Intentionally stepping on another cadet's toes is a strong personal insult, which was obviously here intended.
39 Sel. Docs., Roll 1, pp. 158-162
40 Black Cadets Admitted to USMA", Archives of the United States Military Academy, West Point

CHAPTER 4

Henry Ossian Flipper

After Smith's belligerent refusal to accept the cold racism with which he was treated, formal judicial actions against him resulted, some of which, as they were reported by the press, seemed more like political show trials to justify and reinforce the status quo than anything else. Newspapers watched eagerly for more emotionally charged stories as the procession of African-American cadets continued.[1]

Many of the staff and faculty at West Point had been converted to abolitionist sentiments by the recent Civil War, but many others shared the harsh racist attitudes that were popular across the land. Many from both camps, no doubt, also felt that the Military Academy was not the proper place for social experimentation. Whatever their personal attitudes, in their official dealings with African-American cadets, the faculty and staff were usually precise and correct and did not hesitate to stop or punish white cadets who openly crossed the line too far. However, they made little effort to check what Flipper was to call "these little tortures - the sneer, the shrug of the shoulder, the epithet, the effort to avoid, to disdain, to ignore." [2]

Henry Ossian Flipper was born a slave in Thomasville, Georgia, on March 21, 1856, the oldest of five brothers. He and his mother were the property of a Methodist minister, while his father, a skilled shoemaker, was owned by a slave dealer. An industrious bootmaker and carriage trimmer of some renown, his father was able, even before the Civil War, to conduct a relatively autonomous trade. When his father's master proposed moving to Atlanta and thus separating the family, their great concern was finally resolved in a complex way that seems strange today. Since the father was a slave, whatever money he earned in his trade belonged to his master. So the father paid from his own pocket the purchase money for his wife and son, the sum to be returned to him by the slave dealer - and now the new owner of the wife and son - "whenever convenient."[3]

The details of Flipper's early life and much more are found in his remarkable autobiography, *The Colored Cadet at West Point*, which consists of notes he made as a cadet and later polished, and from which much material here presented is drawn. This profuse recording of his cadet experiences is really unrivaled by any other cadet in West Point history. It seems to be particularly reliable because it appeared so soon after his graduation and all the other figures either named therein or who were at West Point contemporaneously and might have challenged his version of events have failed to do so convincingly. His work has been accepted as accurate and important by scholars since. It is of particular value because of the great detail he provides, not only of particular humbling events he experienced, but more importantly, of his own thoughts and feelings as he endured these strains and attempted to rise above them. But it is also striking because of the particular skill, the splendid wordsmithery, given his humble origins, with which his story is presented. The very words and style he uses are most important, and reveal a great deal about Flipper the man.

Once in Atlanta, young Henry Flipper got his first formal education from another slave, using a Confederate reprint of Noah Webster's *Blueback Speller*. After the war, he was taught by the wife of a Confederate captain, a neighbor who needed whatever humble sums she could earn, even from former slaves. He and his brothers then enrolled in American Missionary Association schools, and in 1869 he entered Atlanta University. He was a student there when he received an appointment to West Point from his congressman.[4] (The steps he went through to gain an appointment have been set forth in Chapter 1.)

Life was difficult at West Point for Flipper. When he arrived in May 1873, he (naturally) roomed with the only other African-American in the Corps of Cadets, James Webster Smith. "In complexion," Flipper said, "Smith was rather light, possibly an octoroon"[5] - which means an individual whose parentage was 1/8 black and 7/8 white. But after Smith left in May 1874, Flipper was truly alone. A key aspect of the African-American experience at West Point in the nineteenth century was the relative solitude these cadets had to endure. Few of them left anything of significance in writing. Flipper, however, wrote two books, the other on his experience in the West after graduation,[6] as well as a number of shorter articles.

The common stereotypes about former slaves were made more readily understandable by Frederick Douglass, the great African- American abolitionist: " Take any race you please, French, English, Irish, or Scotch, subject them to slavery for ages - regard and treat them every where, every way, as property...let them be loaded with chains, scarred with the whip, branded with hot irons, sold in the market, kept in ignorance...and I venture to say that the same doubt would spring up concerning either of them, which now confronts the negro."[7]

Given that he was a slave for the first ten years of his life, Flipper developed a remarkable skill with the written word. In fact, his care in finding just the right term, the aura of grace and gentility in which he presents the world at West Point - a world that, from all the evidence, must have been absolute hell for him to endure - are most impressive. His extreme politeness and adherence to a high intellectual and moral tone in all his writings seem to indicate that he was the product of a wealthy family that had produced a very refined son indeed, an American aristocrat if ever there was one. And yet, the construction of this splendid gentleman was obviously a function of his own hard work and earnest dedication to his own self-improvement, and little more.

West Point clearly represented the highest pinnacle attainable in life when he arrived, and he remained a steadfast devotee of the institution all his life. He knew what he wanted, and he was relentless in his pursuit of that West Point diploma. Possibly because of warnings he received from Smith, but more probably because of something innate to his character, he established a pattern of passive resistance to personal attack that helped him survive, eventually graduate and, from his perspective, win: "We can sometimes, by so living that those who differ from us in opinion respecting any thing can find no fault with us or our creed, influence them to a just consideration of our views, and perhaps persuade them unconsciously to adopt our way of thinking. And just so it is, I think, with prejudice. There is a certain dignity in enduring it which always evokes praise from those who indulge it, and also often discovers to them their error and its injustice."[8]

I believe his writings convey much more than historical facts, and are themselves important evidence of the moral strength and high character he had forged for himself, regardless of whether this happened as a result of or in spite of his West Point education. But they also remind us of his youth, limited experience in life, and naked vulnerability, for despite staring abundant contrary evidence in the face, he easily slipped from high-minded idealism to naive, wishing-it-were-so immaturity: when he writes as follows: "West Point's greatest glory arises from her unparalleled success in polishing these rough specimens and sending them forth 'officers and gentlemen.' No college in the country has such a 'heterogeneous conglomeration' - to quote Dr. Johnson - of classes. The highest and lowest are represented. The glory of free America, her recognition of equality of all men, is not so apparent anywhere else as at West Point. And were prejudice entirely obliterated, then would America in truth be that Utopia of which so many have but dreamed. It is rapidly giving way to better reason, and the day is not far distant when West Point will stand forth as the proud exponent of absolute social equality."[9]

Flipper was not the first political idealist to write such thoughts, nor the last. But in the face of the unending abuse he endured at West Point, such a statement is dramatic evidence of cognitive dissonance on his part, of his not seeing or hearing that which he did not choose to see or hear, that which did not conform to his hard philosophical attitudes about values and principles important to him and their relation to reality.

Flipper had read much about Cadet Smith and his difficulties before he ever left home. Fortunately for himself, Flipper had a much quieter and calmer disposition than did Smith. He was clearly an introvert, a "loner" for most of his adult life, and was much better able than Smith to function on his own under the racial ostracism at West Point.[10]

To say that Flipper was eager to become a West Pointer would be an understatement. Chapter II of his cadet memoir, entitled "Reporting," begins with the following paragraph: "May 20th, 1873! Auspicious day! From the dock of the little ferry-boat that steamed its way across from Garrison's on that eventful afternoon I viewed the hills about West Point, her stone structures perched thereon, thus rising still higher, as if providing access to the very pinnacle of fame, and shuddered. With my mind full of the horrors of the treatment of all former cadets of color, and the dread of inevitable ostracism, I approached tremblingly yet confidently."[11]

Flipper then entertains the reader for several pages with the rude reception visited on all cadet candidates as they arrived and were escorted into the area of barracks to be met by their first, and now suddenly ferocious, upper class cadets. But on the second day, a letter was delivered to his room, from, Flipper would write, "James Webster Smith, the first and then only cadet of color at West Point. It reassured me very much, telling me not to fear either blows or insults, and advising me to avoid any forward conduct if I wished also to avoid certain consequences, 'which' said the writer, 'I have learned from sad experience' would be otherwise inevitable. It was a sad letter. I don't think anything has so affected me or so influenced my conduct at West Point as its melancholy tone. That 'sad experience' gave me a world of warning. I looked upon it as implying the confession of some great error made by him at some previous time, and of its sadder consequences."[12]

As it happens, a third African-American cadet, John W. Williams from Virginia, also arrived at West Point in Flipper's class. Although Williams failed out in French after one semester, he and Smith are only briefly mentioned by Flipper in his book, even though they were necessarily key social figures in his cadet life. Flipper roomed with Smith for his first year at the Academy.[13] It seems somewhat strange, therefore, that, for all the detailed descriptions of the day-to-day cadet experience, Flipper finds so little space for Smith and Williams. Toward the back of the book, he devotes some thirty pages to newspaper articles on Smith and his problems, but there is little else.

Flipper reprints a great number of newspaper pieces throughout the book, as well as schedules, regulations, class notes, cadet traditions, songs, poems, high jinks, and other items that gave fiber to his life at West Point. Some of his selections from the press are quite emotional, and might be considered too overwrought for publication today. But in the wake of a bloody civil war, feelings ran strong, and the future of a formerly enslaved race was a difficult and emotional issue. Some of the articles Flipper reprints are very powerful indeed, as for example the following piece from *The New National Era and Citizen*, which Flipper tells us was the political organ of the colored people published in Washington D.C.: "Now that they [Flipper and Williams] are in, the stiff and starched proteges of the Government make haste to tell the reporters that 'none of the fellows would hurt them, but every fellow would let them alone.' Our reporter seems to think that 'to be let alone' is a terrible doom. So it is, if one is sent to Coventry by gentlemen. So it is, if one is neglected by those who, in point of education, thrift, and morality are our equals or superiors. So it is not, if done by the low-minded, the ignorant, and the snobbish. If it be possible, among the four hundred young charity students of the Government, that Cadet Smith, for instance, finds no warm friends, and has won no respect after the gallant fight he has made for four years - a harder contest than he will ever have in the sterner field -then we despair of the material which West Point is turning out. If this be true, it is training selfish, snobbish martinets - not knightly soldiers.... If the Smiths, Flippers, and Williamses in their honorable school-boy careers can not meet social as well as intellectual recognition while at West Point, let them study on and acquit themselves like men, for they will meet, out in the world, a worthy reception among men of worth, who have put by the prejudices of race and the shackles of ignorance."[14]

Strong words, these, and yes, inspirational, at least in the abstract. But for a seventeen-year-old lad far from home for the first time and surrounded by hostile peers, words must have worn thin fast. When he saw and heard his supposed peers laughing and joking, celebrating the exuberance of their youth together in free moments while ignoring or intentionally insulting him as it pleased them, Flipper must have endured some terribly sad and lonely evenings after Smith and Williams had departed. For Cadet Smith's academic ranking had been steadily slipping, and while he had done rather well when he repeated his first year, ranking 15th out of 66, the following year found him finishing 37th out of 56. During his fourth year, he had ranked in the bottom ten members of a class of 46 in Chemistry, Tactics, Drawing, and Discipline. But worst of all, after the semi-annual examinations held in June 1874, Smith was found deficient in what was called "Natural and Experimental Philosophy," shortened in official documents to "Philosophy."[15]

The Regulations of the U.S. Military Academy describe this course's contents: "This course will comprise: Mechanics.-lst. General classification of the physical sciences...measurements of the masses; densities and weights of bodies; definitions and descriptions of natural forces;...laws of equilibrium and of motion;...motion of projectiles; planetary motions, and the general principles of physical astronomy"[16] In other words, this was a course that we would probably call "physics" today, rather than one involving discussion of abstract theories and ideas. The same Regulations also specify: "At the close of each examination the Academic Board shall report to the Secretary of War...the names of all Cadets who are deficient in studies or discipline, to be discharged, unless otherwise recommended by the Academic Board."[17]

When he learned of his failure, Smith went to Washington and, in the company of Republican Senator John Patterson of South Carolina, asked Secretary of War Belknap to have him reexamined. Belknap refused this request, explaining that Smith had been fairly examined and failed, and that he wanted to fill Smith's slot at the Academy with another young man. Smith next asked to be "turned back" and required to repeat the academic year, as he had earlier done, rather than be dismissed. Once again Belknap refused, saying that the Academic Board had not recommended this, as they would have if this was their desired result.[18]

However, Belknap also sought outside support to defend himself and the Army against charges of unfairness because of racial bias by those at West Point who had examined Smith. On August 3, 1874, he wrote to Professor Francis Wayland of Yale, who had been a Member of the Board of Visitors who had observed Smith's examination, and asked as follows:

"As you were present as a Member of the Board of Visitors at the West Point Military Academy during the last examinations, in June, and were, with them other Members of the Board of Visitors, personally present at the examination of Cadet Smith, of the then 2d class, I would thank you to give me your opinion as to the character of the examination he passed and in regard to his treatment by the examining officer, and the opinion, if you know it, of the other Members of the Board of Visitors concerning the fairness, impartiality, and result of his examination."[19]

On August 8, Professor Wayland replied: " I think that I express the opinions of all the Members of the Board of Visitors who were present at the recent examination of Cadet J.W. Smith, late of the 2d class in the U.S. Military Academy at West Point, when I say that his examination seemed to us to be conducted on the part of his instructors with fairness and impartiality and with a manifest desire to afford him every reasonable opportunity and proper facility for acquitting himself with credit to himself and to the academy....I may add that the Board of Visitors, at one of their sessions, discussed the propriety of embodying their opinion to this effect in a formal resolution, and were only deterred from doing so by the suggestion that such action might be premature & unnecessary."[20]

Smith returned home to South Carolina a bitter man. He had been unceremoniously dumped by West Point after four years of pain and strain, and had little to show for his efforts. He wrote a number of newspaper articles that detailed his experiences at the Academy, many of which Flipper reproduces toward the end of his cadet memoir.[21] They make fascinating reading, and while they only present one side of the story, they may, given the racist attitudes held by most Americans at the time, be quite accurate. But Smith was no longer a cadet, and no newspaper article could change that. He did, however, go on to become the Commandant of Cadets and an instructor of mathematics and tactics at the South Carolina Agricultural and Mechanical Institute at Orangeburg, South Carolina.

Now, in the summer of 1874, Flipper really was alone in the Corps of Cadets. He would remain the only African- American there for more than two years, until the arrival of Johnson C. Whittaker from South Carolina on September 1, 1876.[22] In his cadet memoir, Flipper discusses the solitary nature of his existence, and reveals a lot about himself and the courage that bore him through the four year storm. Ernest Hemingway once defined courage as nothing more than grace under pressure, and Flipper's experiences at West Point certainly met that test. For his was a courage that gave this low-born man nobility and enabled him not only to survive in a hostile environment, but even to win his own moral victories: "But what a wretched existence was mine when all this [social interaction with male and female peers] was denied me! One would be unwilling to believe I had not, from October 1875 until May 1876, spoken to a female of any age, and yet it was so. There was no society for me to enjoy - no friends, male or female, for me to visit, or with whom I could have any social intercourse, so absolute was my isolation. I could and did have a pleasant chat every day, more or less, with 'Bentz the bugler,' the tailor, barber, commissary clerk, the policeman who scrubbed out my room and brought around the mail, the treasurer's clerk, cadets occasionally, and others. The statement made in some of the newspapers, that from one year's end to another I never heard the sound of my own voice, except in the recitation room, is thus seen to be untrue. Indeed, I had friends who often visited me, but they did so only when the weather was favorable... At any rate I can console myself in my victory over prejudice, whether that victory be admitted or not. I know I have so lived that they could find in me no fault different from those at least common to themselves, and have thus forced upon their consciences a just and merited recognition whether or not they are disposed to follow conscience and openly accept my claim to their brotherly love."[23]

Flipper, too, had his toes metaphorically stepped on with daily and almost mind-numbing regularity by other cadets. He recounts many of these occasions, of course, but they are less interesting than the indications he gives of his own psychological growth and the strengthening of his spirit before the howling winds of intentionally bestowed discomfort.

By his third year at West Point, Flipper experienced greater acceptance by other cadets, probably because they no longer feared him as a threat to the traditions of racial dominance that had long flourished there. He had shown levelheaded coolness and composure in the face of serious insults, and was not nearly as aggressive in demanding that he be accepted and respected by other cadets, as Smith had been. He did well academically, and related a number of personal experiences that give the flavor of his still-difficult life as a cadet. Then he defended the path to acceptance that he had chosen: "I am sorry to know that I have been charged, by some not so well acquainted with West Point and life there as they should be to criticize, with manifesting a lack of dignity in that I allowed myself to be insulted, imposed upon, and otherwise ill-treated. There appears to them too great a difference between the treatment of former colored cadets and that of myself, and the only way they are pleased to account for this difference is to say that my good treatment was due to want of 'spunk', and even to fear, as some have said. It evidently never occurred to them that my own conduct determined more than anything else the kind of treatment I would receive.

"I do not mean to boast or do anything of the kind, but I would suggest to all future colored cadets to base their conduct on the golden mean. It is by far the safer, and surely the most Christian course." [24]

This is representative of the high-minded philosophical material threaded through his narrative: it is almost the stuff of promotional material produced by a public affairs office, and yet, from all the evidence, he surely wrote from his heart. He suffered greatly, and yet he presented the Academy in such glowing terms that one is convinced his time there was the central highlight of his life. His work almost seems to exude the philosophical underpinnings on which West Point is based - selfless service to others, principled behavior under pressure, death before dishonor - one can scarcely believe that this idealistic author, a man who seems to out-West Point most other West Pointers, is the same individual who was so badly treated by those other cadets who now seem to have been little more than small-minded thugs and villains.

While still formally ostracized at the beginning of his fourth and final year at West Point, his First Class year, he reported that the insults had lessened dramatically, that some cadets even occasionally spoke to him, though furtively. Meanwhile, Johnson C. Whittaker, an African-American from South Carolina had been admitted in September 1876, and he became Flipper's roommate for that year. Flipper reported: "Shortly after entering [Whittaker] was struck in the face by a young man from Alabama for sneering at him, as he said, while passing by him. Whittaker immediately reported the affair to the cadet officer of the day, by whose efforts this belligerent Alabama gentleman was brought before a court martial, tried, found guilty, and suspended for something over six months, thus being compelled to join the next class that entered the Academy".[25]

So, indeed, things looked a lot different six years after the first African-American cadet had entered West Point. Other changes were also going on at the Academy, changes wrought by President Grant primarily for political reasons. Since 1870, the press across the country had been telling lurid stories about the harsh treatment of African-American cadets at West Point. Most of this treatment had taken place at the hands of prejudiced cadets, young men who were neither more nor less racist than their civilian peers - which meant they exhibited very negative attitudes toward these new arrivals who broke the color line.[26]

Newspaper and magazine reporters soon made it seem there was a conspiracy among staff, faculty, and cadets against the new African-American cadets. At first, to be sure, the staff and faculty had perhaps not been forceful enough in ensuring that cadets abided by the law, as was the case with Cadet James Smith. Once the rumors got out, they quickly spun out of control, and later action to force minimal respect and compliance with the law by cadets did not get much attention in the press. President Grant was embarrassed by these events, and as his Republican party was heavily dependent on the African-American vote, he had to do something.

He finally decided to ask a Civil War hero, Major General John M. Schofield, to take over as superintendent. Schofield was unhappy with the prospect, taking over a position formerly filled by a colonel, a rank two grades below his own. But Grant urged him to accept, assuring him that he would work directly for the only officer who outranked him, the Commanding General of the Army, William T. Sherman. Schofield finally accepted and took over in 1876, the year Johnson Whittaker entered the Academy.[27]

As graduation grew closer, Flipper began to think about his future. When he was commissioned after graduation, he would become the only African-American officer in the army:

"What manner of treatment the cadets chose to manifest toward me [at West Point] was then of course of no account. But what is of importance, and of great importance too, is how they will treat me in the army, when we have all assumed the responsibilities of manhood, coupled with those of a public servant, an army officer. Of course the question cannot now be answered. I feel nevertheless assured that the older officers at least will not stoop to prejudice or caste, but will accord me proper treatment and respect....There is none of the recklessness of the student in their actions, and they cannot but recognize me as having a just claim upon their good-will and honor."[28]

This perception, while high minded, was once again quite unsophisticated. It would only be a few years after his commissioning when Flipper would find himself caught up in-a professionally fatal controversy with fellow officers that, had it not been for his race, probably never would have arisen and certainly would have had an outcome less personally harmful to him. Flipper also discussed the concept of "social equality," which was not a civil "right" to him, but rather something that occurs naturally (and only) between those with similar backgrounds. Despite his very humble origins, Flipper entertained the highest aspirations for himself, and really seems to have believed that, with a measure of grit and determination, his constitutional freedoms would open all social doors to him.

He sometimes seems to have been almost naive in his perseverance, but his positive outlook, as fanned by Radical Republican concepts for former slaves during what must have been, for him and them, the very heady days of Reconstruction after the Civil War, is impressive. Once he got into West Point, he gritted his teeth and endured, becoming in the process perhaps as much of an elitist as any of his fellow West Pointers. He saw education as the key for anyone of any race to raise his station in life, and some of his comments on race bear repeating: "I hope my success has proved that not color of face, but color of character alone can decide such a question [one's fate]. It is character and nothing else that will merit a harsh treatment from gentlemen, and of course it must be a bad character....The whites may admire pluck in the negro, as in other races, but they will never admit unwarrantable obtrusiveness, or rudeness, or grossness, or any other ungentlemanly trait, and no more in the negro than in others. This is quite just. A negro would not allow it even in another...But it is color, [negroes] say, color only, which determines how the negro must be treated. Color is his misfortune, and his treatment must be his misfortune also. Mistaken idea! and one of which we should speedily rid ourselves. It may be color in some cases, but in the great majority of instances it is mental and moral condition…. Color is absolutely nothing in the consideration of the question, unless we mean by it not color of skin, but color of character, and I fancy we can find considerable color there." [29]

Then he gets into the larger question of social equality between the races, a question that necessarily underlies his presence at West Point and, indeed, his entire venture into a social world heretofore untrod by members of his race: "Color is of no consequence in considering the question of equality socially.... Want of education, want of the proof of equality of intellect, is the obstacle, and not color. And the only way to get this proof is to get education, and not by 'war of races.' Equal rights must be a consequence of this proof, and not something existing before it..... And moreover, I don't want equal rights, but identical rights. The whites and blacks may have equal rights, and yet be entirely independent, or estranged from each other. The two races cannot live in the same country, under the same laws as they now do, and yet be absolutely independent of each other. There must, there should, and there will be a mutual dependence, and any thing that tends to create independence, while it is thus so manifestly impossible, can engender strife alone between them.... Therefore I want identical rights, for equal rights may not be sufficient."[30]

In his writings, Flipper could be a compelling and, indeed, a prescient man. He here predicted the ultimate social core reality toward which our nation strives after decades of wrenching national pain caused by U.S. Supreme Court decisions on state laws that required segregation by race, the whole doctrine of "separate but equal."[31] The above section illustrates, I believe, the reason I have chosen to include lengthy extracts from Flipper's writings rather than simply summarize them and present what I believe to be the kernel of his meaning: The very words themselves, given their source, have great import, and a majesty all their own that does not bear smothering, whether by contemporaneous and closed-minded West Point cadets or later observers.

And then, finally, the moment was at hand. On June 14, 1877, Henry Ossian Flipper graduated from West Point, the first African-American to do so. He was ranked fiftieth out of a class of seventy-six, and became West Point graduate number 2,690.[32] Up to this point in his story, Flipper had reproduced a dozen newspaper articles in his cadet memoir and presented all sides to the controversy. When he came to his graduation, however, he reproduced more than two dozen more, again presenting negative stories as well as positive, that related to his final ceremonial receipt of his academic degree and his commissioning into the Army as the only African-American officer in its ranks. None other than General William Tecumseh Sherman, commanding general of the army, led the applause at Flipper's graduation, and many of his class, finally, congratulated him. His class album includes a photograph of him alone, but he is not seen in the group photograph of his class. Flipper was willing and perhaps even eager to rationalize and excuse such petty insults and exclusions, but he should have taken warning for the future when his class staged a minstrel show on the night before graduation.[33]

But Flipper seemed to ignore such evidence, preferring to believe that, by persevering, he could win the other cadets to full and complete acceptance of him. He clasped at the signs and symbols of his class at West Point as if that had, after four years, actually occurred: "The ring is the signet that binds the class to their Alma Mater and to each other. It is to be in after years the souvenir that is to recall one's cadet life, and indeed every thing connected with a happy and yet dreary part of one's career."[34]

He was assigned to the 10th U.S. Cavalry (Colored) in Texas, and a whole new chapter in his life began as his cadet memoir ended. His attitude throughout the book was uniformly humble and self-effacing. One aspect of his grace throughout his narrative was that, whenever an event occurred that might later cast discredit on another individual, he was very careful to omit that person's name, either by leaving a blank or by referring to him as "the Gentleman." He never betrayed any inappropriate self-promotion or even *amour propre*, preferring to let the reader learn of events or experiences favorable to him from the newspaper and magazine story excerpts he reprinted.

Upon graduation, he happily presented the evidence that his endurance had paid off and he had finally been accepted: "Even the cadets and other persons connected with the Academy congratulated me. Oh how happy was I! I prized these good words of the cadets above all others. They knew me thoroughly. They meant what they said, and I felt I was in some sense deserving of all I received from them by way of congratulation. Several visited my quarters. They did not hesitate to speak to me or to shake hands with me before each other or anyone else. All signs of ostracism were gone. All felt I was worthy of some regard, and did not fail to extend it to me.[35] That glorious day of graduation marked a new epoch in my military life. Then my fellow-cadets and myself forgot the past. Then they atoned for past conduct and welcomed me as one of them as well as one among them." [36]

It may seem somewhat surprising, over a century later, that someone badly treated over four years could sound so generous to the very individuals who had scorned him. But that reaction, of course, gives us important insight into both the character of this particular individual as well as the African-American experience at West Point during the nineteenth century. Flipper also went out of his way to thank all who were truly kind to him, starting with those who were too often taken for granted: "Before closing this chapter I would add with just pride that I have ever been treated by all other persons connected with the Academy not officially, as becomes one gentleman to treat another. I refer to servants, soldiers, other enlisted men, and employees.

They have done for me whatever I wished, whenever I wished, and as I wished, and always kindly and willingly. They have even done things for me to the exclusion of others. This is important when it is remembered that the employees, with one exception, are white."[37]

The last paragraph in the book tells much about the steadfast nature of his commitment to West Point and the career of service in the army to which he further aspired: "I have not a word to say against any of the professors or instructors who were at West Point during the period of my cadetship. I have everything to say in their praise, and many things to be thankful for. I have felt perfectly free to go to any officer for assistance, whenever I have wanted it, because their conduct toward me made me feel that I would not be sent away without having received whatever help I may have wanted. All I could say of the professors and officers at the Academy would be unqualifiedly in their favor."[38]

One of the most important things taught at West Point is the importance, and the power, of individual principled behavior under pressure. No matter what the challenge, if one asks oneself what the principle involved is, then the appropriate behavior in response will always become clear. In the words of Epictitus, one must always "do the right thing." Once the principle has been made clear and the individual has taken his stand, then he cannot be defeated; he can be killed, but he cannot be defeated. It would be difficult to contrive individual behavior that would have, under similar circumstances, indicated a higher acceptance of, and commitment to, the principled behavior under pressure taught at West Point than that displayed by Flipper.

When Flipper finally received his diploma and left West Point for service in Texas, he truly believed that he had, by perseverance, finally won his fight for acceptance. He had graduated and been commissioned an officer in the U.S. Army, and at long last had won recognition by his classmates and others at West Point as an officer and a gentleman, an equal and a true professional who was embarking on that same noble profession of arms. But he would serve in a unit whose enlisted ranks were uniformly filled by other African-Americans and whose other officers were all white Americans. He should have anticipated some of the problems ahead. He would not command white Americans in this new role, and his race would be a key component of the unhappy events that would end his military career.

ENDNOTES: Chapter 4

1. Edward M. Coffman, *The Old Army, a Portrait of the American Army in Peacetime,1784-1898*,(New York, 1986) pp.226-229.
2. Henry O. Flipper, *The Colored Cadet at West Point*,(New York, 1878) p.135; Coffman, p.227.
3. Fipper, *Cadet*, pp. 7-8
4. Ibid, pp.11-13.
5. Ibid, p. 287
6. Flipper, Henry O., *Negro Frontiersman: the Western Memoirs of Henry O. Flipper, First Negro Graduate of West Point* (El Paso, 1963).
7. Speech by Douglass at Cooper Union, 12 February, 1862, published in New York Tribune, 13 February, 1862.
8. Flipper, *Cadet*. p. 151
9. Ibid, pp.146-147.
10. Ibid, pp.7-28.
11. Ibid, p.29.
12. Ibid, p.37.
13. Ibid, pp.164-165.
14. Ibid, pp. 46-47.
15. Official Records, Class of 1875, Archives of the U.S. Military Academy, West Point.
16. *Regulations for the U.S. Military Academy at West Point, New York*, Baldwin and Jones, New York, 1866, p.11.
17. Ibid, p.25.
18. Vaughn, p.102.
19. Flipper, *Cadet*, p.164
20. Ibid, p. 167.
21. Ibid, pp.288-317
22. "Black Cadets Admitted to USMA", Archives of the United States Military Academy, West Point.
23. Flipper, *Cadet*, pp. 106-107
24. Flipper, *Cadet*, pp.160-161.
25. Flipper, *Cadet*, p.165.
26. Ambrose, p.233
27. Ambrose, pp.233-234
28. Flipper, *Cadet*, pp.177-178.
29. Ibid, pp.178-181.
30. Ibid, pp. 184-185.

31 The key cases are Plessy v. Ferguson, 163 U.S. 537 (1896), upholding laws providing for racial segregation, and Brown v. Board of Education of Topeka, 347 U.S. 483(1954), finding such laws to be unconstitutional.
32 Official Records, Archives of the U.S. Military Academy, West Point.
33 Coffman, p.227.
34 Flipper, *Cadet,* p.206.
35 Ibid, p 244.
36 Ibid, p.249
37 Ibid, p.161
38 Ibid, pp.321-322.

This illustration from Harper's Weekly (May 1880) depicts the Court of Inquiry considering the case of Johnson Whittaker.

CHAPTER 5

Johnson Chesnut Whittaker

At the beginning of 1877, his last year at West Point, Flipper had been joined by another African-American, Johnson Chesnut Whittaker, a deeply religious South Carolinian who became his roommate. Although Whittaker would experience the same harassment Flipper had, the outcome would be much different.

Johnson Chesnut Whittaker was one of twin sons born on August 23, 1858, to Maria J. Whitaker on the plantation "Mulberry" in South Carolina. Maria was a house slave for Mulberry's owner, James Chesnut, Sr., a leading figure in South Carolina. Maria's husband was a freedman, James Whitaker. (In later years, Johnson would spell his surname with two t's).[1] They also had a one-year-old son, Edward, but James was to abandon Maria because of his suspicion that the twins were not his sons. Before the Civil War, James Chesnut Jr., the son of Maria's owner, was a United States Senator, a man who would become a General in the Confederate army and an aide to Jefferson Davis, President of the Confederacy.

The Chesnut family is probably best remembered because of a diary kept by James Jr.'s wife, Mary Boykin, the famous *Diary from Dixie*. This diary was written from the vantage point of Mulberry, to which Mary Boykin had moved in 1861. It chronicles not only the life of the Confederacy, but also the lives of Maria and her children: Edward; Johnson, the future cadet; and Johnson's twin brother, Alex

Flipper's example had obviously affected Whittaker, for over the next three years, he silently accepted and absorbed without protest the insults and hostile attitudes displayed toward him by other cadets. Another African-American, Charles A. Minnie, was appointed to West Point from New York in September 1877, but after one semester, he was found deficient in mathematics and dismissed, leaving Whittaker to face the storm alone. Flipper had graduated in June 1877, and Whittaker might well have been the second African-American to graduate, but for an incident that occurred on April 6, 1880.[2]

On that morning, Whittaker was found lying on the floor of his room, his hands tied together in front of him, his feet tied to his bedstead. His head appeared beaten, and his ears and scalp were bleeding. He reported that three masked men had entered his room, pulled him from bed and wrestled him to the floor, where they tied him up, beat him and cut him with a knife and cut his hair with a pair of scissors.[3] After his minor wounds had been treated and bandaged at the hospital, Whittaker gave the authorities a handwritten note he said he had found in his room the previous day. The note was in longhand and read as follows:

> Sunday April 4th
> Mr. Whittaker,
> You will be "fixed" Better keep awake
> A friend.[4]

So began what was to become perhaps the most notorious of the racially motivated incidents alleged to have occurred at West Point during the nineteenth century. Whittaker was in his fourth year at West Point by the calendar, but he was in the process of repeating his third academic year. That is, upon completion of the first semester of his junior year, it was determined that he had failed the first semester of the course then called "Philosophy" -- a nineteenth century name for what we today call "Physics," the same academic reef on which James Smith had earlier foundered. Failure of any one course then was ordinarily grounds for dismissal, but the superintendent overruled the Academic Board in this case and caused him to join the following class, thus repeating the second semester of his sophomore year and the first semester of his junior year.

General Schofield, who had become the superintendent at President Grant's urging, found himself in a very difficult position. The results of the immediate internal investigation he ordered had been delivered to him, and had found that Whittaker was the only suspect. It was believed that the note of warning was in his handwriting, and that too many pieces of evidence pointed to his having tied himself up and injured himself, hoping the blame would fall on others and somehow allow him to slip through the final exams, scheduled for June 9th to 11th, which he allegedly feared he would not pass.[5]

The superintendent therefore established a court of inquiry to investigate and resolve the issue for him. The court began its hearings, and every detail was carried in national newspapers. Clever lawyers jousted, handwriting experts testified, and the evidence or lack thereof seemed to be drawing a closing ring around Whittaker. Finally, on 29 May, the court of inquiry delivered its judgment: Whittaker had acted alone and his injuries were self-inflicted.[6]

Whittaker would fail his final examination in the philosophy course on June 11, 1880, but was not discharged or turned back to repeat the academic year because his judicial situation remained unclear. Finally, the War Department informed Schofield that his case was suspended for trial by court martial, convened in New York City on 22 January 1881. But President Rutherford B. Hayes had had enough of Schofield as superintendent at West Point. In December, 1880, he was replaced by General Oliver O. Howard, the single figure who was known to the public as both a valorous general officer crippled by wounds received in the Civil War, and an undeniable lifelong friend of the African-American.[7]

On June 10, 1881, the court martial delivered its judgment: Whittaker had indeed written the note and mutilated himself, the court said, but it eliminated the parts of the charges that said he had performed these acts for notoriety, to bring discredit on the Military Academy, and to avoid the approaching final examinations. The sentence of the court martial was the payment by Whittaker of a fine of $1, his dishonorable discharge from the Military Academy, and confinement in a penitentiary at hard labor for one year.[8]

Upon review by the Judge Advocate General's office, the conviction was overturned on a technicality on 22 March 1882. But Whittaker's failure of that 11 June 1880 examination was used as justification to dismiss him from West Point and allow the authorities to drop him from the rolls.[9]

So ended the West Point experiences of the sixth African-American to be admitted to the U.S. Military Academy, the third to spend more than three and one-half years there as a member of the corps of cadets. It is unfortunate that Whittaker's efforts ended so unhappily, all the more so because he never admitted any guilt, and his trials and ultimate conviction were based on circumstantial evidence. He returned to South Carolina, where he became a teacher and also practiced law and dealt in real estate.[10]

Given the publicity that swirled through the press over this event, it became, by far, the event best known to the public about non-white cadets at West Point in the wake of the Civil War: Of the 21 rolls of microfilm records retained by the United States Archives relating to African-American West Point cadets, eighteen are devoted exclusively to Whittaker, the alleged attack on him, and the ensuing court of inquiry and court martial.

This incident is discussed in great detail by John Marszalek in his book titled *Court Martial*. The Marszalek book is well written, quite balanced, and does a good job of summarizing information about the case. It allows an excellent overview of what was known and what was not known about the condition of Cadet Whittaker and surrounding circumstances on the morning of 6 April 1880.

Marszalek's book was republished under the perhaps more colorful title *Assault at West Point*, which in turn gave rise to a movie that was shown on cable television in 1994.[11] The movie, unfortunately, chose to alter facts in order to firmly imprint on the minds of every viewer that Whittaker was attacked by white cadets, and a massive conspiracy then succeeded in protecting the individual perpetrators of the crime while finding Whittaker guilty of making the whole thing up. And while this may be the way things actually happened, the evidence is all circumstantial and there just isn't enough of it, at this late date, to prove either theory of culpability beyond a reasonable doubt.

The movie takes certain statements by different parties out of context to change their meaning, and it actually changes certain facts to make the story more compelling (e.g., it has the attack occur just days before Whittaker was to graduate, when in fact he had more than a full academic year still before him). But the worst part is the pure fabrication where the movie has Professor Richard Greener, Whittaker's patron and the first African-American to graduate from Harvard, go to West Point during a break in the court martial in New York City, where he confronts a cadet by the name of Louis Ostheim. In response to Greener's queries, Ostheim admits that he is a Jew and as such feels sympathetic to Whittaker. He then tells Greener that certain white cadets had attacked Whittaker, that such information was common knowledge among cadets but was being held in strict secrecy so that Whittaker would be convicted of faking the whole attack upon himself and then be dismissed from West Point.

There was a Louis Ostheim who graduated from West Point in 1883, and Richard Greener was the first African-American to graduate from Harvard. But there is no known record of this meeting between Greener and Ostheim having occurred, and it can only be a pure fabrication by the movie makers. Given the prevalence of strongly negative racist feelings held at the close of the nineteenth century by a large majority of white Americans toward African-Americans, the secrets revealed at such a meeting would not seem at all surprising to anyone having any knowledge at all of the racial climate of the 1880s.

The fact that the meeting didn't happen, of course, may not matter to the people who made this movie, for they are apparently trying to tell a larger story and probably find justification for their expansion of fact in some sort of imagined artistic license. But it should matter. A sizeable number of West Point graduates now claim to know all about the Whittaker story. In their words, "I read the book, saw the movie, I know all about what those white cadets did to poor Whittaker." But they often base confirmation of the attack on Whittaker on elements from the movie that its producers know to be major misrepresentations of what actually happened.

While Whittaker may have been attacked by white cadets, there is also at least as large a probability that it is not what happened, that Whittaker actually faked the attack. Those individuals who are convinced that such an attack did occur are left, as their principal emotional reaction to the story, with a residue of disfavor ranging to contempt for the white cadets of the period who attacked Whittaker, for their peers who may have protected them, and for the staff and faculty of West Point who facilitated the whole criminal endeavor. And while these sentiments may well be deserved, such a diversion of energy and attention can easily cause a reader to lose sight of a much bigger and more important picture.

This series of stories about sequential African-American West Point cadets will show gradual change and amelioration in the conditions confronting them, from the open hostility of the earliest days to the dramatically changed circumstances of the 21st century, where African-American cadets confront circumstances virtually indistinguishable from those confronted by white cadets, certainly as close as it is possible for the staff and faculty to make them. If we are to consider the Whittaker case in that context, it does not really matter more than a century later whether Whittaker was attacked or was shamming, since either (as we shall see) may have been the case. The important issue, no matter what happened, is to look at the causative factors: what kind of country was this in 1880, what kind of society, what kind of culture, that the cream of her young men might either have attacked Whittaker and then denied complicity, or, in the alternative, that they might have driven Whittaker to such a state of desperation that he would have risked everything in an all-or-nothing gamble of such long odds?

As mentioned, Marszalek's book gives a good overview of what happened, and it is most impressive as one's first exposure to this particular set of events. Indeed, after reading Marszalek, but before I learned any more details of these controversial events or of the two trials that ensued, I was (and remain) very sympathetic to Whittaker and the enormous challenges he accepted by stepping forward to become one of the first African-American cadets at West Point.

After reading Marszalek's book, one can only be greatly offended that such a shameful event took place at West Point and that neither the corps of cadets at the time, nor the staff and faculty, were able to determine and punish which cadets had attacked Whittaker. Everything Marszalek says about the abuse and social ostracism Whittaker suffered from other cadets purely as a function of his race rings true. It seems, therefore, that Whittaker was the victim of one of the most wicked and destructive conspiracies in American history, apparently engineered by an otherwise honorable-seeming group of some 250 select young men - West Point cadets. This is all the more interesting because, as Marszalek tells us, Whittaker was so light in complexion that he could easily have passed for white.[12] At one point, Marszalek even tells us that "in a parade or at a distance his race would have been difficult to notice. His hair was not kinky and his light-skinned face was covered with freckles. He was probably no more than one quarter black."[13]

But I found it more difficult to accept that all the white officers at West Point were similarly so heavily prejudiced against him as to be willing to go out of their way and even act unfairly in their efforts to bring about his dismissal from West Point. After all, these events occurred only fifteen years after the end of the Civil War, in which many of these officers had served. Weren't most of these officers Republicans, and wouldn't many of them have still retained strong abolitionist sentiments, which were also those of the Radical Republicans who had wielded enormous political power in Congress since the Civil War, to the point of regularly passing laws favoring freedmen over the vetoes of President Andrew Johnson? Imprudent youth is often the source of great misfortune, but to ask one to believe that mature Army officers were somehow guilty of the same bias strains credulity; somehow, it just doesn't sound right.

As I read, I also noted a few statements Marszalek made that, on the face of them, were clearly inaccurate. For instance, although most of the chapters in the book contain copious footnotes, for Chapter 11 there is only one footnote for the entire chapter. [14] This group of records covers many hundreds of pages. Without more specification, I was unable to confirm from the above-mentioned archival records a section I found in Chapter 11 of Marszalek's book. That section reads as follows: "[Defense Counsel] Chamberlain retraced the role of the five government experts back to the court of inquiry to show their lack of consistency. During their first inquiry testimony, Gayler and Paine could not give a positive opinion because, they said, the note of warning had so little writing on it. Hagan said Whittaker had written the note; Ames said either Whittaker had written the note or it was a 'skillfully executed simulation of Whittaker's writing'; and Southworth said No. 27 was the writer. In short, the preponderance of the evidence was favorable to Whittaker." But even if the content of that paragraph is accurate, the last statement, presumably by Marszalek ["In short, the preponderance of the evidence was favorable to Whittaker"], on the face of it, simply cannot be true.

Webster's New World Dictionary defines "preponderance" as follows: "the condition of being preponderant; superiority in amount, weight, power, influence, importance, etc.". We are told that two experts could not give an opinion on who the author was because there was too little writing on it, one said it was definitely written by Whittaker, one said it was either written by Whittaker or was a skillfully executed forgery of his writing, and one said that the note had been written by "No. 27" (another cadet).

Writing samples from all cadets were examined by these five experts. Two of them say there is not enough writing on which to base a judgment. But in that case, such assessments are not "favorable" or "unfavorable" to Whittaker - they are simply non-assessments, and so are not considered. We are then left with three assessments, one of which says it was Whittaker, another said it was either Whittaker or a skillful forgery of Whittaker's handwriting, and the third said it was another cadet. How, then, can Marszalek say "the preponderance of the evidence was favorable to Whittaker"?

Since we are told that Chamberlain, the defense counsel, traced the opinions of the experts back to their court of inquiry testimony, perhaps a section of the court of inquiry records bears quoting here: "The evidence of the Experts in handwriting is given as to the writer of the note of warning.

This note was submitted in succession to five different Experts, together with specimens of the hand-writing of each Cadet in the Corps [all West Point Cadets], and numerous lecture notes by the members of the 2nd Class [Whittaker's class, those cadets he would have been in classrooms with every day]. In all cases, the identity of the writer was unknown to the Experts, and no Expert was aware of the hand-writing in which any previous one had discovered resemblances to the note....In this severe trial, the 1st, 3rd and 4th Experts, without their knowledge united in indicating Cadet Whittaker as the writer of the 'note of warning.'

"All the Experts except the 3rd were recalled, and specimens of the writing of Cadet Whittaker and of the person selected by the 5th Expert were given to them. They were then unanimous and emphatic in the statement that Cadet Whittaker wrote the note of warning. One of the Experts also discovered evidence proving satisfactorily to the Court and to the counsel of Cadet Whittaker that the paper upon which the note of warning was written had been torn from a sheet upon which Cadet Whittaker had written the first part of a letter to his mother, dated April 5th 1880.[15]

In the six-page final chapter to his book, entitled "Conclusion," Marszalek makes his feelings plain: "West Pointers were convinced Whittaker had committed the attack on himself to aid the Academy's enemies and to gain revenge for cadet ostracism. The possibility of anyone else committing the act, especially other cadets, was never seriously considered despite the recent memory of the successful New Year's Eve escapade. West Point's racial prejudice and its concern for itself precluded such a consideration. The Academy acted from bias and fear."[16]

That's a strong, adversarial statement, and it would be more expected from one of Whittaker's defense lawyers than from an historian attempting to retain some semblance of objectivity. We will return to this paragraph at a later point, but Marszalek was deeply caught up in his sources, and his intimacy with the pertinent material may well have caused him to come down on one side of such a sharply drawn issue. And clearly, he felt deep sympathy for Whittaker, however subconscious it may have been, all along. In the "Afterword" to the book, Marszalek discusses the early days of his research on this subject. He says that, when he visited the National Archives with his wife and they first held Whittaker's bible with the flowers pressed between its leaves, "We stared a long time at that bible and those flowers, Whittaker's spirit passing through to us across the suddenly loosened barrier of time."[17]

At a later point, he talks of visiting Whittaker's grave in Orangeburg, S.C.: "I spotted a large monument and walked toward it. I saw the word: 'Whittaker.'. Below it: 'Johnson C.' Through the trees I could see a storm gathering on the horizon; the sun cast a shadowy spotlight on the gravestone. An electric sensation passed through my body. I had found him. I stood motionless for a long time trying to take it all in, trying to experience the moment in every way I could. I thanked God for bringing me there. I promised Johnson Whittaker's spirit I would write this book."[18]

At first blush, that sounds like he then intended to write a book that would show only one side of the story, how Whittaker had actually been attacked by white cadets and in so doing, somehow redeem his reputation from wrongful conviction by two courts of having feigned the whole affair. Fortunately, some reassurance that he will not be blind to the truth can be found in his blunt statement on the last page of the "Afterword": "My job as a historian is to present the truth about the past in the most objective way I can, and I believe I've done that in *Assault at West Point*."[19]

Marszalek's book seems quite balanced and objective, though he clearly believes, given all the evidence on both sides with which he is intimately familiar, that there was an assault made against Whittaker by white cadets that was then denied and covered up. The very change in the title of the same book, from *Court-Martial* in 1972 to *Attack at West Point* in 1994, makes that abundantly clear. And even historians are entitled to their own opinions on controversial issues such as this one, especially someone as deeply knowledgeable of the details as is Marszalek.

In his "Conclusion", Marszalek even gives us his own beliefs on the issue of which version of the events of the early morning hours of April 6, 1880 was accurate: "Did Whittaker really commit the nighttime attack himself and then try to shift blame onto West Pointers? There is no conclusive proof of Whittaker's guilt. The facts are circumstantial and his life before and after was blameless - in fact, in many ways exemplary. He might have suffered a momentary aberration, but this seems doubtful. The facts of the case do not justify a guilty verdict, and his entire life makes his guilt improbable."[20]

We know that either a group of white cadets attacked Whittaker in his room or that he feigned that attack. As stated earlier, it does not matter, for this work, whether the attack occurred or was feigned by Whittaker: Either possibility is understandable and evokes great sympathy for Whittaker, no matter what happened. But in the interest of historical accuracy, it seems important to look once again at the paragraph that appears on page 275 of

Marszalek's book. If it sounds like an adversarial paragraph that would more likely have been written by one of Whittaker's defense lawyers than by an historian. In the interest of objectivity, some balancing response is required.

In the first sentence of that paragraph, Marszalek places himself inside the mind of "West Pointers" (presumably those cadets and members of the staff and faculty then at West Point) and not only tells us what they "were convinced" - that Whittaker had committed the attack upon himself - but also why they "were convinced" he had done it: In order to aid the Academy's enemies and to gain revenge for the social ostracism he had endured.

It may well be, of course, that the great bulk of West Pointers at the time, upon consideration of the evidence that was brought out at the court of inquiry and the court martial, became convinced that Whittaker had fabricated the attack. But Marszalek says they were convinced he fabricated the attack in order to help the Academy's enemies and to gain revenge for the cadet ostracism he had experienced. Those seem spurious grounds on which anyone would base such dramatic actions: that "West Pointers" would believe a cadet would tie himself up, cut his ears and chop his hair, miss formation, feign unconsciousness, and fabricate a fantastic story about a night attack on the top floor of the cadet barracks by three strangers in civilian clothing - all to help the Academy's enemies and gain revenge for ostracism.

Whittaker was finishing his junior year, and no doubt hoped to graduate, as Henry Flipper had a few years earlier. He was a West Point cadet now and, upon graduation, would become a fully fledged member of the "Long Gray Line" (an appellation of West Point graduates much favored by themselves): Why would he want to help the Academy's "enemies," since he stood only to gain in life from his membership in such an elite number? And would anyone really take such dramatic steps, including the risk of being found out and dismissed from West Point, just to "gain revenge for cadet ostracism"? Why does Marszalek seem to be hanging on such a weak straw? Was there no other credible motive for Whittaker to have fabricated the whole story?

The other sentences of this paragraph are equally confusing. The reference to the "New Year's escapade" seems illusory at best, for the entire scale is different: The fact that cadets might not voluntarily turn in other cadets who had set off fireworks on New Year's eve, with no harm done to anyone, does not mean that, if Whittaker had been beaten by cadets, they would not turn in the guilty parties. The possibility of other cadets having made this attack certainly was considered seriously by the authorities at West Point, but the evidence left in Whittaker's room pointed relentlessly at him. No other individual cadet was ever found to be even remotely connected to the events of that night.

A review of the records leads me to believe that the West Point authorities and, indeed, most members of the corps of cadets, initially did believe Whittaker's story and continued to do so at least until the commandant of cadets, Major Henry M. Lazelle, delivered the formal report of his first investigation on April 8, 1880, finding Whittaker alone culpable and resulting in the court of inquiry. Lazelle's first report was delivered at 6 p.m. on April 8 - some 62 hours after Whittaker was found tied to his bed. But news of Whittaker's situation on April 6 spread like wildfire on this small military post, and within hours, everyone had heard about it. I have not seen anyone's expressed opinion during the first few days that was not sympathetic to Whittaker, and many that were, expressed both by cadets and officers. After Lazelle delivered the results of his investigation, however, events began to appear from a different perspective.

Thus, Marszalek's statements that "West Point's racial prejudice and its concern for itself precluded" any serious investigation into white cadets having attacked Whittaker, and that "The Academy acted from bias and fear" sound like what someone seeking emotional support for his charges of criminal action on the part of whites against blacks in 1880 might say, charges that happened to be politically popular in the United States a century later. But a careful reading of the records of both trials will not lead to quite such a clear view of what actually happened.

In attempting to verify Whittaker's story, the only evidence we have is what was found in the room, and in reviewing that evidence, let us use Marszalek's version. He first tells us that Whittaker was absent from reveille on April 6, 1880. A cadet sent to his room found him lying, inert and unconscious, on the floor next to his bed. His feet were tied together and bound to the bedstead with cut-down white cloth cadet belts, and his hands were bound together in front of him with the same type of belts. Tying his feet to the bed was certainly possible, as were cutting his hair and ears. But what of tying his hands in front of himself? This sounds like a very difficult if not impossible task for an individual by himself. I therefore contacted the West Point supply officer and was able to secure a set of the white cotton dress belts that cadets have used since before the Civil War. I then cut them in half lengthwise ("cut-down belts" means flat cotton belts normally two inches wide that have been cut down to only one inch in width) and attempted to tie my wrists together in front of me. I found that, using my teeth as well as the fingers of both hands, I could do this very easily: in less than a minute, I was able to tie the belts so tight that I had to get help to remove them.

Then Marszalek describes Whittaker: "Whittaker was all covered with blood. There was blood on his face, his neck, his ears, on one of his feet, on the shoulders of his undershirt, and on his drawers above the knees. There was also blood on the center of the mattress, on the wall above the middle of the bed, and on the floor. Some of the material found on the floor near Whittaker was stained, as was the doorjamb. The pillow was soaked with blood."[21]

That sounds like a bloody massacre had taken place. After such an introduction, one would expect Whittaker's wounds to have been grievous and perhaps even life-threatening. But the next paragraph describes his wounds, and they seem less than expected: "Whittaker's right ear was slashed across the lobe, causing a wound five-eighths of an inch long, with a slighter cut just above the first. The left ear had a small piece of the lobe cut off. There are two five-eighths-inch parallel cuts on the little toe of his foot and a scratch and a non-bleeding abrasion on his left hand."[22]

According to Marszalek, then, the bleeding wounds Whittaker suffered were two half-inch cuts on one little toe, two more on one ear, and a "small piece" of the other ear lobe cut off. That hardly seems enough to account for all the blood described in the first paragraph: "Whittaker was all covered with blood...The pillow was soaked with blood."

The Court of Inquiry report gives us some insight on the seriousness of the wounds:

"The pillow was much stained with blood. There was also blood about his hair and ears, and on his shirt at the shoulders; there was a little blood on the legs of the drawers above the knees, a little upon his feet, and some upon the bands attached to his ankles and wrists. There were several spots of blood upon the floor near his body, a little upon the underside of the mattress at the foot, and upon the upper side at the head. There was a stain of blood on the wall of the room about over the middle of the bed."[23]

The same report describes Whittaker's wounds at a later point: " The personal evidences of an assault were: incised wounds on the anterior surface of the lobes of both ears, about 5/8 inches long on the right ear, not so long on the left; also an exceedingly small piece removed from the tip of the left ear; a cut resembling a pin scratch across the back of the left hand; two cuts, very slight, and about 5/8" long, across the top of the little toe of the left foot. The Surgeon estimated that from 11/2 to 2 ounces of blood [3-4 teaspoons] had been lost....The hair at the back of his head was cut in swaths, extending from the back of the right ear around and upward to the left. The hair had also been cut in spots on the left side, on top, and a little from the right side. No other injuries, bruises, or marks whatever were found upon his person, and at 11 o'clock that day he attended his usual recitation."[24]

Apart from the minor disagreement between these sources over whether both ears were slashed 5/8 of an inch or just the right ear had two such slashes, these two descriptions are similar. But it is important to remember the lightness of Whittaker's skin, else the absence of any bruises, welts, or other marks of serious blows might be attributed by the unwary to the presumed darkness of his skin.

The perverseness of these racial standards when considered at the start of the twenty-first century, and their impact on individual lives, is shown by part of a *New York Times* article that gave some background on the Whittaker investigation at West Point: "A circumstance which lends additional countenance to the belief that the outrage was committed by three Cadets is the fact that Whittaker, wittingly or unwittingly, has given offense to several members of the corps who are not the sort of persons to forget injuries. Besides the Alabama Cadet, McDonald, who struck Whittaker twice on slight provocation, and was suspended a year in consequence, the Cadets say that there are two boys who have an especial cause of grievance against the young Negro. These boys, it is said, came to the Point to pass their examinations at the same time as Whittaker. The latter, who is freckled and whiter than many of the white Cadets, neglected to tell the others that he had a strain of dark blood in his veins, and all three roomed together and ate at the same table. The horror and disgust of the young Caucasians on discovering that they had associated on terms of equality with a "white nigger" was so great that Whittaker's perfidy became a byword among his fellows. Flipper, who was undeniably black, got along better, as there could be no mistaking his color."[25]

Given what we have already seen of Flipper's solitary existence for four years, it is difficult to accept that he "got along better," unless it was meant by this that he escaped anything like the attack of April 6, 1880. But race was still determined, in those days, according to rigid standards that had to do with the presence of African blood in one's body rather than one's shade of skin or physiognomic features. These standards were left over from the days of slavery, but they endured well into the twentieth century. For instance, in a 1923 letter to his nephew, Henry 0. Flipper referred to his grandmother as an "octoroon."[26] This means that she was, by parentage, 1/8 black and 7/8 white - but she was still classified as an African-American. Given that her daughter (Henry Flipper's mother) was a slave, she was probably a slave herself. Indeed, in the slave markets of New Orleans and other southern cities, octoroon women brought high prices, indistinguishable in appearance, as they often were, from white women.

Marszalek has in that way recaptured the true spirit of the time. He finds a deep antipathy held by virtually all whites at West Point for African-Americans. Stephen Ambrose makes the same point: "Throughout the Reconstruction period the treatment of Negro cadets was a popular subject for newspaper and magazine reporters. Generally the treatment implied that there was a conspiracy at West Point, one which included not only the cadets and faculty but the army as a whole, to ostracize the Negroes. In point of fact there was no conspiracy, for there was no need for one. Prejudice against Negroes was neither higher nor lower at West Point and in the army than it was throughout the nation - which meant that it was high."[27]

Marszalek's book presents an event that was replete with emotion as stories for and against Whittaker surged through newspapers across the country. On one side was a young man whose skin color, facial features, and hair type were apparently indistinguishable from those of a white youth, but who was considered a black, and as such, became one of the first of his race to take on the challenges of West Point; on the other, a school that claimed, but failed, to extend equal treatment to cadets of all races. It failed because, while the legal portion of the bargain may have been performed, the social portion was ignored. On the all-important human and social level within the corps of cadets, then, there was no official direction or control from above, and this absence of authority probably spoke louder than any possible words: black cadets were roundly reviled by white cadets. It is therefore not unreasonable to infer that unconscious motives may have driven the authorities at West Point to allow the travesty of finding all white cadets innocent and Whittaker guilty of having staged an attack upon himself. This is the situation made abundantly clear by Marszalek.

Unfortunately, he does not fully develop the other side. His book really does not develop or explain the motive found by both the court of inquiry and the court martial to have been sufficient for Whittaker to have falsely alleged such an attack and to have prepared evidence sufficient to make his story believable.

A section of Marszalek's book will perhaps show what I mean: "He finished that year [his sophomore year] successfully but the following January [1879] ran into difficulty. He failed an examination and was slated for dismissal. Fortunately for him the Superintendent, General John M. Schofield, gave him and two white cadets the opportunity to repeat the year rather than be dismissed. In Whittaker's case, Schofield said that he was influenced by Whittaker's hard-working determination and the fact that he was the only black cadet at the Academy. Consequently, the academic year 1879-1880 found Whittaker repeating his second-class (junior) year instead of being a member of the graduating class.

In summary, Whittaker could be described as a quiet young man with average academic achievement. Even though he was repeating subjects in 1879-1880, he remained in the bottom half of his class. In March, 1880, he dropped into the sixth, or last section in the nineteenth century equivalent of physics, natural and experimental philosophy. But, according to later statements of the head of the philosophy department, Colonel Peter S. Michie, he was in no danger of failure. Michie called him a 'very studious and very attentive' student whose memory was 'excellent.' His over-all average for the repeated year was about 83%." [28]

Unfortunately, that's not an accurate picture. First of all, though three cadets in that class failed philosophy in January 1878, only Whittaker and one other cadet were allowed to repeat the academic year: the third cadet, though he ranked higher than Whittaker, was not seen to have as studious a nature and was dismissed. The third cadet on whose behalf Schofield successfully petitioned the secretary of war and won him the right to repeat an academic year was not one of those who failed philosophy with Whitaker; rather, he was a member of the class behind that of Whittaker and Hammond and was thus junior to them. And Whittaker's "over-all average" is really irrelevant, for failure of any single semester-long course was then grounds for dismissal from West Point.

But the actual quotations attributed to Michie, of Whittaker being "very studious," "very attentive," and having an "excellent memory" are accurate:

> Q. Did you find him always a studious and attentive scholar?
> A. Very studious and very attentive...
> Q. What would you say of his memory for instance?
> A. His memory is excellent...[29]

Later, the Court asked Michie to clarify his testimony:

> Q. Do you mean by your testimony in cross examination that the ability of the accused to remember what was carefully explained to him indicated the requisite capacity for what was called a difficult subject of study?
> A. I do not.[30]

That last comment seems somehow to dilute Michie's earlier high regard for Whittaker's memory, but the other statements are rather naked and stand somewhat alone. What we must realize, however, is that this court martial testimony follows that which Michie gave at the court of inquiry, and depends on it as a base. Indeed, much of the questioning of Michie at the court martial asked if he still felt the same way he did at the court of inquiry, repeating to him his testimony there, in which he uniformly concurred. In order to understand Whittaker's academic situation, then, one needs some of Michie's testimony from the court of inquiry:

> Q. Please state to the Court as fully as possible your knowledge of Cadet Whittaker as regards his Academic history and present status - Academic status, general capacity as a student and the chances in your opinion of his getting through his present academic year?
> A. Cadet Whittaker came into my department...in September 1878... and during the succeeding four months of that session his tendency was downward, and finally at the examination in January, in my opinion he was deficient...and by my recommendation to the Academic Board of his deficiency, he was so declared. He was recommended for discharge and...the recommendation was unanimously acceded to by the Academic Board but the Superintendent in opposition to that recommendation recommended to the Secretary of War that he be granted another trial, and he with one of his companions was accordingly turned back into the third class....He came again into the department of philosophy in September 1879, and going over these subjects again he succeeded, coming out I think 41 in a class of 59. ...Immediately after the January examination, starting upon a new subject of acoustics, optics, and astronomy...Cadet Whittaker has gradually

gone down in his class rank, and I think now stands 4 from the foot in his aggregate in this class....I regard Cadet Whittaker as being a very studious cadet but of very little aptitude indeed, and I think that if he had been a white cadet he would not have progressed as far as he has.... His reasoning power is not up, I think, to our average. Those are my views with regard to Cadet Whittaker after a careful study of his case for a year and a half.[31]

So while it is true that Michie used the specific words cited by Marszalek, if we look back to the context of those statements, they take on an entirely different meaning. He also said that, had Whittaker been white, he probably would not have gotten as far as he had - apparently a reference to Superintendent Schofield's overriding the Academic Board in January 1879 and turning him back a year. In his letter to the Secretary of War requesting permission to turn back Whittaker and two others, Schofield said: "In the case of Whittaker, I do not know but I may be influenced somewhat by the fact that he is the only one of his race now at the Academy, and has won the sympathy of all by his manly deportment and earnest efforts to succeed. The Professors do not think he can ever master the course, but I am disposed to give him another chance."[32]

Was Whittaker really in academic danger? Did his fall to the sixth section give any warning of academic danger? As discussed in Chapter I, the sections at West Point are ranked on a curve, and as each week's grades are accumulated, the membership of the sections gradually changes, so that, over time, the more intelligent cadets tend to accumulate in the higher (lower numbered) sections, while the less intelligent cadets tend to fall toward the lower (higher numbered) sections. Here, the 6th section in Philosophy was the lowest, and each semester, one or more cadets in the lowest section of Philosophy were liable to fail the course and be dismissed from West Point on those academic grounds alone.

To understand his academic situation, we need to consider the testimony of Whittaker's primary classroom instructor in Philosophy, Captain Clinton B. Sears, at the court of inquiry:

Q. Have you ever been an instructor of Cadet Whittaker?

A. I have been an instructor of Cadet Whittaker at two different times continuously.

Q. Please make a statement telling all you know with reference to the official Academic history of Cadet Whittaker as a student, and chances of getting through his present year?

A. As I have said, Cadet Whittaker was under my instruction for fully four months the first time. Previous to the January examination 1879 when I came to sum up the marks of my section in philosophy...Cadet Whittaker and two other Cadets were found deficient...The reason that Cadet Whittaker was found deficient was not from want of study or application, but I think from a want of intellectual power to grasp the subject. It is perhaps the most difficult one here, being the application of the higher mathematics to a large extent, requiring a good deal of reasoning power and a pretty thorough knowledge of some applications of mathematics. He was one of the most attentive, and as far as I could judge from his recitations one of the most industrious cadets whom I have ever had under me... As a result of examination Cadet Whitaker's industry and good conduct he was turned back, I believe by the recommendation of the Superintendent, into the next class....When asked my opinion about being turned back I remember now that I made this remark "He should be turned back in preference to the others, still from my knowledge of his reasoning powers and his intellectual grasp I have considerable doubt that he will be able to get through and I do not think it will be very long...before he will be back in the last section." [33]

Let us next look at some more of Professor Michie's testimony from the court of inquiry:

Q. Has it been customary in your department to regard a cadet in the last section as in danger?

>A. We regard cadets in the last section as being in a dangerous position.
>
>Q. Do you think the Cadets clearly understand that?
>
>A. It used to be so considered when I was a Cadet, and I presume it is so now. The last section has the title of "immortals," and that means that a man will have to study very hard and do very well in order that he shall succeed in passing his examination.
>
>Q. It is not customary to inform the members of that section that they are in danger?
>
>A. It has been customary, and that caution is always given in my department to the last section, that they are in danger and that they must do the very best they can and I have always given instructions and always had them carried out that any cadet who has any difficulty in his study on subject should make that difficulty known before recitation began in order that full and complete information might be given him, so that by no possibility he shall say that he was unable to obtain the necessary information.[34]

And finally, let us look at one last piece of testimony from Captain Sears at the Court Martial:

>Q. On the 5th of April, he was not in what you would call a dangerous position?
>
>A. Oh, yes; he was in a dangerous position.
>
>Q. Why?
>
>A. Because he had been going down....
>
>Q. If the examination had taken place on the 5th of April he would not, had he kept up to the point where he then was -- he would not have been thrown out?
>
>A. Not if he had kept the same position.
>
>Q. Then what you call his "dangerous" position is based upon the idea that he would continue to sink?
>
>A. Yes, and the fact that we were then getting into the most difficult part of the course. As we professed, he was going down. In a doubtful place they will give him a

much closer examination. If not doubtful they may not give him an examination particularly close. But I had expressed my doubt as to his being able to get through before this occurred -- based upon my knowledge of his position.[35]

So we have seen that, although Michie did say Whittaker was "very studious," "very attentive," and had an "excellent" memory, he also found him to have very little aptitude and to lack the reasoning power necessary for success at West Point. Michie said he thought Whittaker would pass the final test (though he reserved the right to change this opinion later), while Sears said he did not believe that he would. Both said that he was in a very dangerous position in the bottom section, and Sears said that his grades up through 5 April -- he day before the attack -- were heading precariously downward.

Marszalek does not develop the opinions of Michie or Sears, beyond summarizing a few words from Michie at the court martial that mislead the reader into thinking Michie had a very high regard for Whittaker's academic competence. But when counterpoised against his comments in the court of inquiry, and when added to the comments of Captain Sears, a wholly different view emerges of Whittaker and his precarious academic position.

Sears was the recorder at the court of inquiry, and as such filled a role much like that of a prosecutor in a criminal trial. And given his official adversarial role, it may be that this stance caused his testimony to be biased against Whittaker. But that does not justify ignoring or suppressing it. Who could have a better appreciation of the academic situation of a young man who is in danger of failing a specific subject than the man who taught that subject to him in the classroom?

And if prejudice was suspected on the part of Sears, that was addressed by him in the opening section of the "Remarks of the Recorder" in the final report of the court of inquiry: "When I was first assigned as the Recorder of this Court, I was as truly without an opinion as to the merits of the case as could have been desired in any juryman. As I have announced in Court, I was personally without an opinion to express, or a theory to support. I had read little and heard still less. Equally was and am I without prejudice against the colored race as a race. A republican in sympathy and an original abolitionist in education, I could not consistently be otherwise than justly and kindly disposed towards the negro, and it was a pleasure for me to be able to testify as I did to the character and standing of Mr. Whittaker. If, then, in my subsequent remarks I appear to bear heavily on him, it is because my official duty demands, and the great weight of the testimony justifies it."[36]

Similarly, if one reads only the quotes Marszalek has selected from the court martial records, then Whittaker seems to have been on firm academic ground. But if one reads more from both the court martial and the court of inquiry proceedings -- as anyone researching this case in any depth would certainly do -- then those simplistic comments are clearly misleading.

It is possible, of course, that Michie, the head of the department of Philosophy, and Sears, his classroom instructor, were both racially biased against Whittaker and wanted him to fail for that reason, their sworn testimony to the contrary notwithstanding. Perhaps their maintenance of his academic records over more than a year and all their testimony in both courts were calibrated to bring about his dismissal. However, the complexities that would have necessarily been involved in such a conspiracy lead one to look for a simpler answer.

So it appears, then, that Whittaker did have a motive - fear of academic failure, a potential that loomed large before him and may well have pushed him to take desperate steps like feigning this attack. Why? Perhaps in the hope of arousing sympathy at West Point and across the nation so that, if he did fail Philosophy, sympathetic professors might give him the benefit of the doubt. And if he failed to arouse their concern enough to do so, a sympathetic Congress might step in, a sympathetic President.... who knows? And even if his efforts failed, at least he would arouse the sympathy of those already in his corner, and his departure from West Point would be, for them, made in a blaze of glory rather than as a function of a silent administrative dismissal from West Point for academic failure. Was that motive enough for Whittaker to have performed some truly desperate act of deceit? If he feared that his dream of becoming the second African-American to graduate from West Point was about to disappear because of his inability to master complex mathematics, then his options might well have become those of desperation.

Indeed, if Whittaker did make up the whole thing, his motivation would be easily understandable today. *Black's Law Dictionary* is commonly used by American lawyers for definitions and reference. The first definition of "duress" found in that dictionary is "Unlawful constraint exercised upon a man whereby he is forced to do some act that he otherwise would not have done," [37] and any black cadet in the 19th century who might have been caught constructing such a ruse just to stay at West Point could arguably have claimed duress as a defense. Given societal attitudes at the time, however, the racist behavior of white cadets would probably not have been seen to be "unlawful". But more than a century later, an objective observer is not so eager to condemn Whittaker even if he did feign the attack. Indeed, there might even be at least grudging admiration for someone who had reacted to this racist isolation with such creativity under pressure and, ultimately, strong personal courage.

The ultimate question of whether Whittaker was attacked by a cabal of racist cadets who were then protected by the West Point bond of silence to outsiders, or Whittaker feigned the whole thing out of desperation, will never truly be known. The racist tenor of the times, the far more serious violence occasionally enacted on one another by cadets, and the strong personal ties among cadets that could easily have fended off intrusive outsiders, these speak strongly to the first option. But there is more weight than Marszalek is willing to admit behind the possibility that Whittaker created the whole issue as a desperate diversion - specifically, that Whittaker did have a motive driven by his proximate academic danger.

This is a complex case and the records are long and confusing. Whittaker had a plausible motive for faking the attack and once that dimension is developed, one sees the whole case from a slightly different perspective. Unfortunately, Marszalek seems driven to present the story in a light uniformly favorable to Whittaker. He emphasizes the centrality of racism at West Point. The real problem of Whittaker's life was not academic. It was the fact that, like the black cadets who had come before him, he was completely ostracized by the cadets and staff at West Point. No one spoke to him except on official business and then as briefly and usually as curtly as possible. Cadets reproached him if he tried to sit next to them at the mess table or if he tried to fall in next to them at formation. It was reported that one cadet was willing to give up his corporal's stripes rather than stand in formation next to the black cadet. On one occasion another cadet, George Burnett, took a command which was supposed to be Whittaker's. A cadet named Blake got into an argument with Whittaker when Whittaker took his hat by mistake after a meal. No one would room with the black cadet, so, once Flipper and Minnie were gone, Whittaker had to himself a room normally occupied by two cadets.[38] Yet despite this treatment, Whittaker - like Flipper - might well have graduated from West Point and gone on in life despite these painful personal experiences.

Unless we are willing to believe that Schofield, Michie, and Sears were all lying in their sworn testimony and had altered the records to make Whittaker look bad academically, then there is another, "real problem" here, one which presented a much more immediate threat to his continuation as a cadet at West Point.

The real "real problem" for Whittaker at the time had nothing to do with social atmosphere. Rather, it was an "all or nothing" future he faced academically: Unless he was somehow able to succeed academically -- to pass the final examination in philosophy that loomed before him unavoidably -- he knew he would be forced to leave West Point, not because he was liked or disliked by others, but rather because he was unable to keep up academically in accordance with supposedly color-blind standards. And at West Point, the curriculum then (and until late in the twentieth century) was prescribed, and failure of any single course meant automatic dismissal. Occasionally, cadets were allowed to repeat academic years after failure. Whittaker had already used this mechanism once; it must have been abundantly clear to him that he would not be able to avail himself of it again. Schofield was even asked about this possibility at Whittaker's Court Martial:

> Q. Do you know of any instance in the course of your tour of service at the Military Academy, of a cadet having gone over a course the third time?
> A. I have not heard of any such instance.[39]

In the twenty-first century, it is both easy and appropriate to be sympathetic to Whittaker and the trials and tribulations he underwent at West Point. Whether the attack occurred or Whittaker falsified the whole thing is far less important than the fact that others deemed it possible.

Newspapers from across the country were at first ravenous for news about this event, and their appraisals over time truly ran the spectrum. But even so, one article from the *New York Times* of the period captures what one must, more than a hundred years later, consider to be among the fairest and most balanced things that were said about this case: "[W]hether he was really subjected to violence or not, his treatment during his whole experience at West Point has been in the spirit which might have prompted it. He has been looked upon as an inferior. Everybody appears to have avoided all association with him and endeavored to make him feel that he was socially degraded and unfit for the company of the "high-toned gentlemen" around him. His isolation must have been depressing and discouraging to the last degree.[40]

Clearly, Whittaker, like all other black cadets who had preceded him at West Point, was socially ostracized by his white peers. Unhappily, rather than becoming the second African-American to graduate from West Point, he was sacrificed on the altar of racial prejudice and fell by the wayside. And this racial sacrifice occurred whether he was the subject of a physical attack on the night of April 6, 1880, or was driven to invent and feign it. No matter the origins of this event, Whittaker's inability to stay the course at West Point was primarily a function of the virulent racism then coursing through the land. But however slowly, for those African-Americans who followed in Whittaker's path, progress would eventually come.

ENDNOTES: Chapter 5

1. John F. Marszalek, *Court-Martial*, (New York, 1972), p.28.
2. Coffman, p.227; "Black Cadets Admitted to USMA", Special Collection, U.S.M.A. Archives, West Point, N.Y.
3. The Proceedings of the General Court Martial of Johnson C. Whittaker, United States Military Academy, Records of the Judge Advocate General (Army), National Archives Record Group 153, QQ2774, Part XV, pp.1224-1246, hereafter cited as W.C.M. Records.
4. Ibid, pp. 1282-1291.
5. Ibid, pp.1224-1292.
6. The Proceedings of the Court of Inquiry in the Case of Johnson C. Whittaker, US Military Academy, Records of the Judge Advocate General (Army), National Archives pp. 2806-2817; hereafter cited as C of I Records
7. John Marszalek, *Court Martial* (New York) 1972. pp 137-154
8. Ibid, pp. 238-239.
9. Ibid, pp.248-249.
10. Ibid, pp.255-273.
11. *Court Martial* was originally published by Scribner's in 1972, then republished by Macmillan under the title Assault at West Point in 1994. The movie, based on Marszalek's book, is titled "Assault at West Point" and was first shown on *Showtime* in February 1994
12. Marszalek, pp.38, 278.
13. Ibid, p. 67
14. "1. The Summations of Daniel H. Chamberlain, Defense Counsel, and Asa Bird Gardiner, Judge Advocate, discussed in this chapter may be found in Parts LXVIII to LXXII of the Proceedings of the General Court Martial of Johnson

15 C. Whittaker, United States Military Academy, Records of the Judge Advocate General (Army), Record Group 153, QQ2774, National Archives.
15 C.of I. Records, pp.2810-2811.
16 Marszalek, p. 275. The "New Year's Escapade" refers to a prank-- the explosion by cadets, against regulations, of fireworks on New Year's Eve 1879-1880-- and the inability of West Point authorities to find and punish those responsible
17 Ibid, p.283.
18 Ibid, pp. 286-7.
19 Ibid, p. 289
20 Ibid, p.276
21 Ibid, p.45
22 Ibid.
23 C. of I. Report, frame 339.
24 Ibid, frame 342.
25 *New York Times*, April 17, 1880.
26 Flipper to "Dear Nephew", 10 June, 1923, Special Collections, U.S.M.A. Archives, West Point, N.Y.
27 Ambrose,p.233.
28 Marszalek, pp.40-41.
29 W.C.M. Records, pp. 1535-1536.
30 Ibid, p.1545.
31 Ibid, pp.2009-2012.
32 Letter dated January 15, 1879, to Secretary of War from Major General J.M. Schofield, Superintendent, U.S. Military Academy; USMA Archives, West Point, N.Y.
33 C. of I. Records, pp.1973-1982.
34 Ibid pp. 2016-17.
35 W.C.M. Records, pp. 1432-34
36 Sel. Docs., Roll 7, frames 209-219
37 Henry Campbell Black, *Black's Law Dictionary*, 4th Ed., (St. Paul, MN, 1968), p.594.
38 Marszalek, pp. 41-43
39 W.C.M., pp.132-134.
40 *New York Times,* June 14, 1880

Chapter 6

The Fight Endures

Henry O. Flipper graduated from West Point in 1877, and in 1878, Flipper's memoir of his days at West Point, *The Colored Cadet at West Point*, was published in New York by Homer Lee & Co. Thus, by the age of 21, Flipper had earned a degree from West Point, was finishing his West Point memoir, and had orders to head for the frontier, where he would command United States cavalry troops and play a role in the white settlement of the West.

The 10th Cavalry Regiment, commanded by Colonel B.H. Grierson, was one of the four all-black regiments (9th and 10th Cavalry, 24th and 25th Infantry Regiment) in the U.S. Army. Flipper's first posting was with "A" Troop (a military unit of a hundred-odd soldiers, called a "Company" in the infantry, is called a "Troop" in the cavalry) at Fort Sill, Indian Territory (Oklahoma). Flipper took up his duties in January 1878, and as the only African American officer in the entire U.S. Army, his social circumstances were no doubt strained. He denied that, as had been predicted in the New York Tribune, he would be more alone in his regiment than he had been at West Point: " From the moment I reached Sill, I haven't experienced anything but happiness. I am not isolated. I am not ostracized by a single officer. I do not 'feel it more keenly,' because what the *Herald* said is not true. The *Herald*, like other papers, forgets that the army is officered by men who are presumably officers and gentle-men. Those who are will treat me as become gentlemen, as they do, and those who are not I will thank if they will 'ostracize' me, for if they don't, I will certainly 'ostracize' them."[1]

Happy words these, and surely more optimistic and upbeat than circumstances warranted. For Flipper was soon to be rudely awakened to the fact that not all of the officers of the U.S. Army were yet willing to accept an African American, no matter how intelligent, competent, and well-educated at the "right" school, as their full equal.

For several years after his arrival, Flipper's unit moved around to different U.S. Army forts in Texas and Indian Territory while fighting Indians and/or outlaws. In the spring of 1880, "A" Troop arrived at Fort Davis, Texas, where it had been transferred with two other troops of the 10th Cavalry in order to fight Victorio's hostile Mescalero Apaches. Fort Davis was less than sixty miles from the Rio Grande, and after a brief stop there, "A" Troop took up the chase of Victorio and his men, along with several troops of the 8th (white) cavalry and a company of Texas Rangers.[2] Fierce fighting resulted in the deaths of nineteen Indians and three troopers. Flipper was designated to read the Episcopal service over the troopers, who were buried where they fell, after which a volley was fired and the buglers played taps. Then at the end of November 1880, Flipper and "A" Troop returned to Fort Davis.[3]

Without judging the moral or ethical rectitude of these American soldiers fighting these Apaches, I think it important to recognize that Flipper here risked his life, under arms, for his country. One is reminded of the words allegedly inscribed at Thermopylae: "Stranger passing by, go and tell the Spartans that we lie here, obedient to their laws." Or perhaps, more pointedly, the words of Robert E. Lee: "A call to serve one's country is a high call; a call to serve her under arms in time of war is the highest." Given the great hardships Flipper had suffered to win his commission, he probably would have preferred to have died on the high plains, felled by a hostile bullet, than to have to bear the unanticipated and unwarranted court martial and disgrace awaiting him.

In early December 1880, Flipper was made Acting Assistant Quartermaster and Acting Commissary of Subsistence at Fort Davis. These staff duties were usually filled for short periods by designated junior officers. Flipper put a most positive light on what he clearly saw as an opportunity to excel rather than a burden to bear: "I had charge of the entire military reservation, houses, water and fuel supply, transportation, feed, clothing and equipment for the troops and the food supply."[4]

Such administrative jobs are more tedious than complex. The junior officers filling them are generally supported by sergeants below them who are familiar with the routine and senior officers above them who watch to make sure that young officers avoid blunders. Flipper, unhappily, was to commit some youthful blunders, but without the kindly oversight of a concerned superior officer who might have guided him painlessly back to solid ground.

Because of the particular nature of his position as the only African American commissioned officer in the United States Army, he held himself, and was held by others, to a higher-than-normal standard of conduct. That standard was of almost superhuman proportions, and the nature of his social environment precluded senior officers or even his peers seeking him out with advice or assistance. It also prevented Flipper from sharing the confidence of, or seeking counsel or support from, his fellow officers. Thus, truly alone and somewhat innocent in administrative or financial matters, to say nothing of the cloaked cupidity of his fellow man, Flipper seemed destined to trip one day, sooner or later, and take a hard fall.

Because of his commissary responsibilities for buying and selling foodstuffs and other goods, Flipper gave credit to enlisted men and others when he shouldn't have and soon found himself in over his head. As the charges against Flipper grew and his eventual trial by court martial proceeded, it will be noted that there are numerous inconsistencies, some due to the varying ways of calculating, others apparently due to actual differing charges. But the basic financial situation was this: Flipper fell behind in payments due to the Army's Commissary fund for as much as $3700. This was due in part to his allowing members of his Troop to run up debts to him, and then he himself charged these and his own debts to the Commissary fund.

In addition to whatever role latent racism may have played – a significant force -- it seems his problem was also due in part to his own faulty bookkeeping. It could also, although suspected but never proven, be a function of thefts from his footlocker where he kept the Commissary fund cash. Eventually, Flipper was able to come up with some mislaid checks and repay his debt -- but that was mostly thanks to civilian friends who contributed the bulk of the repayment, some $2300. All other calculations and sums will be little more than distracting, and are largely irrelevant.

Flipper's social life in Texas was certainly strained. His Troop Commander, Captain Nicholas Nolan, was a widower over fifty years of age with two small children. As soon as "A" Troop was established in quarters at Fort Sill in 1878, Nolan went to San Antonio, where he wooed and wed Annie Dwyer. He brought his bride back to Fort Sill, and her sister Mollie came along. Nolan insisted that Flipper eat with them, and he did. Mollie and he became what he called "fast friends", and soon enough, they were going on long horseback rides together.[5]

This is an instance of what can only be termed incredible naiveté on the part of Flipper. He believed the army to be led by officers and gentlemen who would not "ostracize" him, and if they were so intolerant as to be unable to accept him on that basis, he preferred them to keep their distance. He tried to live according to those rules, fully acting out the role of a West-Point-graduate-commissioned-officer, assuming all the rights and responsibilities to which he believed he was thus entitled. He tried to pay no attention to officers prejudiced against him, but they were legion, and surely he was not ignorant of their feelings.

For instance, while "A" Troop was at Fort Elliott, Texas, the wife of one of the other officers wrote to Eastern newspapers criticizing Nolan and his wife for receiving and entertaining Flipper in their quarters. In response, Captain Nolan wrote a letter of protest that was published in *The Army and Navy Journal*. This publication made a practice of reprinting official orders, excerpts from court martial proceedings, and other military news items during the late nineteenth century, thus capturing the flavor of the social and military life of the officer corps. In Nolan's letter, he admitted his bias in favor of Flipper because, as a much-persecuted Irishman himself, he felt he shared a bond of persecution with African Americans.[6]

Flipper resumed his rides with Mollie Dwyer at Fort Davis in December 1880, but a new Lieutenant, Charles E. Nordstrom, arrived. In a few words from his frontier memoir, a rigidly correct Flipper only hints at what must have been his broken dreams, and the galling hell of Nordstrom's proximity. For even if his relationship with Mollie Dwyer was truly nothing more than a platonic friendship, he had precious few of those to spare. Flipper would write: "and we got Charles E. Nordstrom as 1st Lieutenant. He also came from the Civil War Army, was a Swede from Maine, had no education and was a brute. He hated me and gradually won Miss Dwyer from her horse back rides with me and took her riding in a buggy he had.... He married Miss Dwyer after I was dismissed."[7] Sadly, this story only makes Flipper's efforts to defy longstanding tradition seem destined to fail.

In the spring of 1881, Fort Davis changed dramatically. Until that time, the fort had been commanded by Major N.B. McLaughlen of the 10th Cavalry. During the months of March and April, all the cavalry units except "A" Troop were dispatched to other posts, and the headquarters of the 1st Infantry arrived, commanded by Colonel Rufus Shafter, who also took over command of Fort Davis. Shafter's regimental adjutant, 1st Lieutenant Louis Wilhelmi, relieved the post adjutant, and his regimental quartermaster, 2nd Lieutenant

Louis Strother, relieved Flipper as the post quartermaster. Shafter told Flipper that he would also be relieved as Acting Commissary of Subsistence as soon as possible, that he might devote his time fully to his role as a cavalry officer, but that he would retain the position for an indeterminate period while personnel were shifted around. He ended up retaining the job until August 11 when he was replaced by Lieutenant Frank H. Edmunds.[8]

Meanwhile, Wilhelmi was a familiar face from Flipper's past. Several years older than Flipper, Wilhelmi had started his military career as a cadet at West Point in 1872, but he fell ill during his first year and started again in 1873, this time with Flipper's class. The sickness returned, and he left West Point for good at the end of 1873. He recovered and was commissioned a 2nd lieutenant in 1875 then was appointed regimental adjutant, a post for which he was promoted to 1st Lieutenant in 1880. Thus, when he arrived at Fort Davis, although he outranked Flipper, the latter had the cachet of a West Point degree, and thus a far superior military education as well as vastly superior potential political power within the army.[9] That potential, however, as we shall see, was largely diluted because of Flipper's ethnicity.

In fact, there were at least five other West Point graduates at Fort Davis who were either Flipper's classmate or had graduated within a few years of him either way. Ordinarily, on a lonely frontier post, West Pointers would have been the fastest of friends, and they have historically maintained a sort of "insiders' club" that, coupled with their traditional dominance of the higher ranks in the army, has long caused considerable bad feeling and resentment among officers who did not graduate from West Point. Though he did not graduate, his time at West Point would have included Wilhelmi in this closed circle. But for Flipper, a freed slave and an African American, this social world remained almost as closed to him in the army as it had been at West Point.

The old "silence" from West Point days was back again - the institutional message, broadcast in the past to Flipper and all other African American cadets by the entire Corps of Cadets: "We do not want you here, and despite the national governmental authorities that have appointed you a cadet, we refuse to recognize your presence and will do everything we can to force you to leave." And now some of his fellow officers on a remote Western post were sending him the same message.

This would soon become formally recognized when, in November 1881, Flipper found himself facing literally the greatest trial of his life: a general court martial. Commissary funds hadn't been turned in for months – where were they? This was Flipper's responsibility, and he had fallen behind by seemingly innocent negligence, coupled with a trusting nature. But instead of paternal guidance from older officers, or even from senior sergeants who knew the ropes, Flipper met blank stares and demands for funds that had been entrusted to him. And when he couldn't come up with the money, he was charged with embezzlement and briefly jailed. Even though he would be able to accumulate enough money to repay his debt within weeks, he first had to face trial by court martial. We will now glance briefly at that judicial event mid-course, when Wilhelmi was asked if he knew Flipper (who had been his West Point classmate):

> Q. Did you know Mr. Flipper personally?
> A. No, sir.
> Q. Never spoke to him?
> A. No, sir.
> ....
> Q. When did you come in contact with Mr. Flipper after leaving the Point?
> A. March of 1881.
> Q. What have been your relations with him here?
> A. They have been of a friendly character.
> Q. Friendly in what respect -- social character -- any relations excepting those of an official character?
> A. That is about all.[10]

This social shunning of Flipper was common. In his *Negro Frontiersman*, Flipper describes an occasion where he ran into a West Point classmate in a strange town: "I went into the San Javier Hotel one day in Tucson for dinner. Lieut. R.D. Read of the 10th Cavalry and a classmate of mine was then at a table. As soon as I sat down he got up and went out without his dinner."[11] Read was in the 10th Cavalry with Flipper at Fort Davis and, before that, at other frontier posts. But when they ran into each other unexpectedly in a strange town, Read's reaction was not only not to ask Flipper to join him, or even to ignore him - he got up and left. So the army's racist mentality to which Flipper had first been exposed at West Point was not dead once he left that institution.

At first, such slights must have been very hurtful indeed, but after four years of it at West Point, followed by five years in the frontier army, it seems Flipper had come to expect such treatment. Flipper, of course, was very popular among the African American enlisted soldiers who filled the ranks of the 10th Cavalry. But the barrier of rank made an impenetrable wall between them socially: even had the disparity of education and experience not been enough to keep them apart, the rigid rules of the army precluded social fraternization between officers and the enlisted ranks.

So Flipper was largely alone socially, as far as the official army was concerned. In his small quarters, he kept a violin, an early typewriter (he had, after all, already written a book that was being commercially published and from which he was awaiting royalties), a "student's lamp," three albums, and 79 books,[12] so he clearly had developed ways to fill his frequent solitary moments. But he also gravitated to the town that had sprung up outside Fort Davis, befriending many of the European American, African American, and Mexican civilians who lived there. His best friend was probably W.S. Chamberlain, a watchmaker, whom he apparently visited every day, with whom he often went on rides and other social outings, and in whose company he often ate his meals. He was also close to Joseph Sender, a merchant whose store, Sender & Seidenborn, was the largest in town.[13]

At his court martial, both Sender and Chamberlain had only the highest praise for Flipper, a man they described as being of the highest personal honor and integrity. But most important, when the chips were down and Flipper needed financial help, they were able to come up with more than $2,000 in loans to him personally from the civilian community at Fort Davis within a few days. That matter will be discussed in more detail at a later point, but it seems to be a reliable measure both of friendship and of a man's reputation in a small community.

Though his service as quartermaster had ended in March, Flipper continued to serve as the post commissary, with an office and a storehouse. Most of the details of buying and selling food for the soldiers and families at Fort Davis were taken care of by Commissary Sergeant Carl Ross, who recorded sales, prepared letters and receipts for Flipper's signature, and generally kept the books in order.[14] Flipper's duties were primarily those of passing on instructions, taking responsibility for all funds received, and the efficient management of the commissary service. All foodstuffs were purchased from the commissary by the soldiers at the post or their families. Officers were allowed credit, usually paying their accrued debt by check periodically, but soldiers were supposed to present cash at each transaction. Each week, the total amount of money on hand, in checks and specie - American and Mexican bills and coins - was tallied and approved by the post commander. Each Saturday, Sergeant Ross prepared these forms for Flipper's signature, which Colonel Shafter, in turn, signed on Sunday morning. A copy of the Statement of Funds was sent to the Chief Commissary of Subsistence of the Department of Texas in San Antonio, another to the Commissary General in the War Department, Washington, D.C., while a third copy stayed in the post commissary office records. The funds themselves were to be sent to San Antonio as soon as practicable after the end of each month.

From March through May 1881, Flipper performed his duties as post commissary in what was certainly more than a satisfactory way; given the racist walls that surrounded him, he had been truly professional and without the slightest fault. Colonel Shafter, the commander of Fort Davis acknowledged this at the court martial: "I found Mr. Flipper, as far as I could observe, always prompt in attending to his duties - performed them intelligently and to my entire satisfaction."[15] His regimental commander, Colonel B.H. Grierson would also provide a most positive appraisal of Flipper, which was introduced at his court martial: "During the entire time specified, his veracity and integrity have never been questioned, and his character and standing as an officer and a gentleman have certainly been beyond reproach.... Being, as an officer, the only representative of his race in the army, he has, under circumstances and surroundings the most unfavorable and discouraging, steadily won his way by sterling worth and ability, by manly and soldierly bearing, to the confidence, respect, and esteem of all with whom he has served or come in contact. As to Lieut. Flipper's late trouble, or alleged offense for which he is now being court-martialled, I have no personal knowledge, but from all information I have been able to gain relative thereto, although he may have been careless and indiscreet, and may have committed irregularities from want of experience, my confidence in his honesty of purpose has not been shaken, and my faith in his final vindication is still as strong as ever." [16]

As we begin to consider the actions for which Lieutenant Flipper would find himself ultimately driven from the Army in disgrace, it is important to recognize the particularity of his position in certain ways. As the only African American officer in the army, he saw the social conditions of others in a way that European American officers did not. His sensitivity for the plight of, and resultant charity toward, those who filled more menial roles at Fort Davis than he did was a source of great confusion, and ultimate disaster, in his own personal commissary debt.

Flipper was especially sensitive to the plights presented by the accident of birth to other peoples of color who had not been so fortunate as himself. An obvious place where he could make their lives incrementally less difficult was in the purchase of foodstuffs from the commissary. Since he was an officer, he could buy on credit, while enlisted personnel had to pay cash. Though his pay as a 2nd Lieutenant was only $125 per month, Flipper made it a custom to allow the African-American enlisted men, laundresses, and others to buy from the commissary stores, drawing on his own credit for payment but keeping little or no record of such transactions. He eventually allowed others to spend on credit in "his" commissary an amount that, when combined with his own modest requirements, came close to consuming all his pay.[17]

At his court martial, his counsel, Captain Merritt Barber, pointed this out: "Look at the condition of his personal accounts, as illustrated by his monthly purchases from the commissary, steadily running up from $72.08 in December to $262.20 in July. Open hearted and not realizing upon what shoals and quicksands he was drifting, generous to a fault, every one who came to him got what they asked, so that during the eight and one half months he was commissary his personal account was $1121.71, at least half of which he thinks is still outstanding, and there is scarcely a scrap of paper or a memorandum of any kind to show how much is owing to him or who owes it."[18]

Flipper's problem surfaced in May 1881 when he discovered that he did not have as much on hand in the form of cash and checks as he should have had. By the end of May, he was short some $800, and he began to alter his reports to his post commander to reflect the amount he had on hand rather than the amount he should have had, while he continued to list the larger amounts on reports to San Antonio and Washington, D.C. At his trial his attorney commented on this: "It was simply a matter with himself and all there was of it, Lieut. Flipper, 10th Cavalry, did not pay his commissary bills to Lieut. Flipper, A.C.S.[Acting Commissary of Subsistence]...He knew there was considerable lacking, and he knew there was considerable due from him to make it up, and as the funds and weekly statements were not to be transmitted for some time, he made the statements to correspond with the actual cash on hand and held himself responsible to pay his commissary bills when it became necessary to transmit the funds. That some person had begun at this time to visit his trunk and carry off money would seem probable." [19]

This reference to "some person" visiting "his trunk" and carrying off money brings up another central issue: the way Flipper kept the commissary funds of which he was custodian. In his statement to the court, Flipper said: "The funds for which I was responsible I kept in my own quarters in my trunk, the trunk I procured at West Point and have used ever since I entered the service. My reasons for keeping them there were that as far as I was responsible for their safety I felt more secure to have them in my own personal custody."[20]

One wonders immediately why Flipper didn't seek to keep the funds in one of the two quartermaster safes. The only mention he made at trial of why he kept the funds in his trunk appears above. But in 1898, he attempted to have Congress intervene in his behalf, and submitted a statement in which he commented on why he kept the funds at home: "When I was relieved from duty as Quartermaster I had no secure place to keep the commissary funds, and so reported to Colonel Shafter. He expressly told me at that time to keep them in my quarters that they would no doubt be safe there for a few days until he relieved me and I turned them over to my successor." Colonel Shafter denied all knowledge of this interview.[21]

The information on Colonel Shafter's role in Flipper's troubles is mixed. It is true that he had Flipper's quarters searched and had him arrested on the flimsy pretext of having seen his saddled horse on the street in town carrying saddlebags,[22] although his horse was always so saddled and Flipper often rode into town during the day or evening. Let us assume for a moment that he did tell Flipper to keep the funds at home. But even given that, if a would-be thief knows his target's location, he still must have physical access to it. And there was no indication throughout the trial that anyone had broken into the trunk in which the funds were kept.

But whether Flipper was ordered to keep the funds in his quarters or simply decided to do that himself, it was a highly imprudent act, given that there were official safes that he might have used. And no matter how secure the trunk itself and its lock may have been, there was at least one other person who had access to the keys and so the contents of the trunk: Lucy Smith. An African America herself, Lucy was Flipper's servant, and she claimed to sleep in a room at one Mrs. Olsup's house in town.[23] There was evidence that she may have been Flipper's mistress as well as his servant, although apparently the morality of the time precluded mentioning this relationship at trial .(She is called "Lucy Flipper" or "Mrs. Flipper," in the trial transcript at least four times, and each time the slip was hurriedly corrected.) But she kept her clothing and personal possessions in Flipper's trunk, which seems to imply more than just the convenience to her that he stated: " My servant having no place to keep her clothing safely had asked me if she could put some of it in that trunk and I granted her permission; keeping the keys myself, and only handing them to her when she desired to get something out or put something in, and then but for a short time; cautioning her to be very careful of my goods and papers and to never leave anything unlocked or insecure." [24]

Lucy's connection to him was clearly more than the normal master-servant relationship one might have expected. In defending his client against the charges of embezzlement, his attorney, Captain Merritt Barber took it upon himself in his summation to refute certain rumors: "The next was the theory that my client had been touched by the tender passion and his heart melting under the gentle influences of a first love had lavished the gold of government on the object of his passion in gorgeous presents of jewelry and attire. But alas for that theory, upon investigation we find he has been guilty of presenting his servant girl an old gold ring which he didn't want and was of no use to her." [25] However "old" and "unwanted" by either of them, what are the circumstances which cause a young bachelor West Point graduate, the black lieutenant adrift on his chosen sea of white officers, all senior to him, to give a gold ring to his black female servant? What was going on here?

In early May, Flipper got a message from San Antonio telling him not to send funds in until June,[26] and during this period, Flipper simply stopped the weekly examination of funds. Weekly reports were prepared during this period by Commissary Sergeant Ross and signed by Flipper, but were not signed by the commanding officer, Colonel Shafter, or his designee in his absence.[27] Shafter did not inspect them again until 8 July. When Flipper prepared his records for the Colonel on 7 July, he found that he was now some $1440 short. So he wrote a check that was to be drawn on his account at the San Antonio National Bank, for $1440.43, [28] even though he had no account in that bank. He showed this to the colonel on 8 July, and with that increment, the other figures tallied for the preceding fiscal period at $3,791.77.

After the 8 July inspection, Colonel Shafter told him to submit the $3,791.77 to San Antonio. Flipper agreed to do so, and ordered Sergeant Ross to make out the invoices and receipts of the funds, which he did. Flipper took them with him, then returned on 10 August and ordered Ross to make out a letter of transmittal for these funds, which he also did. Flipper signed these papers on 11 August, which was the day that, in conformity to Shafter's promise since he had taken over in March, Flipper was relieved as Acting Commissary and replaced in that role by Lieutenant Edmunds.

Flipper had hoped to collect a large amount from soldiers in "A" Troop who owed him money from their credit purchases in his name. "A" Troop came back to Fort Davis on 10 July, but for confused reasons he was unable to make any such collections. He then contacted the Homer Lee publishing company in New York and asked them to send his royalty check to the San Antonio National Bank. He was expecting to receive some $2500,[29] an amount sufficient, once deposited, to cover his check for $1440, which he could then submit to San Antonio and thus negotiate, but the weeks dragged by with no word from New York. Without having forwarded the funds he had secured, he signed three consecutive weekly reports, on 9, 13, and 24 July, all falsely indicating that the $3,791.77 was in transit to San Antonio.

Flipper would explain his actions to the court: "As to my motives in the matter alleged in the first specification of the second charge [having written the check for $1440] I can only say that some time before I had been cautioned that the commanding officer would improve any opportunity to get me into trouble, and although I did not give much credit to it at the time, it occurred to me very prominently when I found myself in difficulty; and as he had long been known to me by reputation and observation as a severe, stern man, having committed my first mistake I indulged what proved to be false hope that I would be able to work out my responsibility alone and avoid giving him any knowledge of my embarrassment."[30]

When the royalty check finally arrived on 17 August, it was too small and too late: Only $74.00, and by then Flipper had been arrested.[31] Major Michael P. Small, the Chief Commissary in San Antonio, had begun pressing for the money. After several messages to Flipper that drew no response, he informed Shafter, first by mail, then by telegram, that he had received nothing.

Initially, Shafter just suspected the normal "slows" of all matters administrative. Then, as time passed, he said, he began to consider foul play. On 10 August, he confronted Flipper, who assured him the checks and currency were in the mail. But more telegrams came in from San Antonio and by this time Shafter said he didn't believe that Flipper had sent the checks to San Antonio. So he ordered Flipper's quarters searched by Lieutenants Wilhelmi and Edmunds. He told them to arrest Flipper if they found "anything suspicious."[32]

They found nothing "suspicious," but they also did not find the commissary money in checks and currency they thought Flipper had retained. They put a guard on Flipper, then returned to Shafter, who told them to go back and make a more thorough search.[33] Then Shafter interrogated Lucy Smith, Flipper's servant. She played dumb, but almost by accident, Shafter discovered that she had two envelopes concealed in her dress. He forced her to produce them, and one contained some $2800 in checks (including the

$1440 check Flipper had written on the San Antonio bank), the other a mass of invoices and receipts.[34]

It seems improbable Lucy was trying to steal them since she would not have been able to negotiate them; rather, it looks like she was just trying to conceal them for Flipper, as he had signed reports and told the colonel that they were in the mail to San Antonio, thereby trying to buy time to cover his missing funds. But now, things looked bad for Flipper. Colonel Shafter had him placed in the guardhouse and told Flipper he believed that he had stolen the difference between the $2300 in checks recovered and the total liability of $3700.[35] Two days later, he learned that Flipper did not have an account at the San Antonio National bank, which made the check he had written for $1440 (included among the $2800 in checks Shafter had found on Lucy's person) worthless. Shafter went to the guardhouse and informed Flipper of this, that his total liability had now risen from $900 to some $2300 or $2400.

Their conversation, according to Shafter, went as follows: "He said, 'Yes, Colonel, I had to deceive you in some way and took that way to do it.' I then said 'You need not criminate yourself, I don't want you to do so unless you choose to, but I would like to know where that money has gone to if you are willing to tell me' He said "Colonel, I don't know where it has gone to". I said 'It is very strange that you should be short $2400 and not know where it is.' He said 'Yes, that is so, but I can't account for it unless some of them have stolen it from me.' I said 'who do you mean by "some of them"? He said 'I don't know.' I said 'Do you think that woman at your house has it or any of it?' He said 'No, sir, I do not.' He said then that if he could see three or four of his friends in town he thought he could make his deficiency good. I said 'Do you think you can make the whole $2400 good?' He said 'Yes, I think I can.' "[36]

Shafter then had Flipper arrested and held in a small (6'6" x 4'6") cell in the guardhouse for four days. The only other inmates were enlisted black soldiers from the 10th Cavalry, who were held in an adjoining large room, in which they were free to move around and interact. Flipper's cell was separated from the enlisted prison room by a wall, and communication was also barred by the social wall that separated officers from the enlisted ranks. But the enlisted men were fully aware of Flipper's presence and the public shame that went with his being held in the guardhouse. Such treatment would have been unheard of for any white officers. Normally, an officer in similar circumstances would have been simply restricted to his quarters, unguarded, while the charges against him were investigated, but for the only black officer in the army, such treatment should not have been surprising.[37]

When Shafter sent news of the affair, of his arrest and confinement of Flipper in the guardhouse, up the chain of command to Headquarters, Department of Texas in San Antonio, the immediate response from his commander, General Christopher C. Augur, was to take Flipper out of the guard house. But the telegram was delayed and didn't arrive for four days. After that, Flipper was restricted to his quarters, where an armed guard was posted.

Some of Flipper's friends from town had visited him in jail, including Chamberlain and Sender. By the fourth day, they were able to come up with a total of $2300, which they gave to Flipper, who in turn gave it to Colonel Shafter. This, combined with the $1400 in "good" checks found on Lucy cleared up Flipper's liability to the government and gained him his release. Shafter contributed $100 to this amount himself. It should be noted, however, that his expressed sympathy is at least suspect since he insisted on retaining Flipper's watch (already in his possession, as were all of Flipper's personal possessions, collected and catalogued by Shafter's order at the time of Flipper's arrest) as collateral for what he would later refer to as his "loan" to Flipper.[38]

But the game was not yet over: On 29 August, Flipper was served with the formal charges filed against him by Shafter. He would have to face a court martial. Flipper asked for a month's delay in order to allow him time to secure the services of a civilian lawyer from New York. This delay was granted, and Flipper negotiated with a lawyer in New York who ultimately declined to act as his attorney in this case. When the court martial formed, Flipper was defended by Captain Merritt Barber, who, on short notice and on what was then literally the wild frontier, did what can only be described as an excellent job.

The court martial took place at Fort Davis in November and December 1881, before a board of ten officers; a "Judge Advocate," Captain John W. Clous (a sort of military prosecutor with enlarged powers); and Captain Barber, Flipper's defense attorney. There were two charges: The first was that he had embezzled $3791.77; the second charged him with Conduct Unbecoming an Officer and consisted of five specifications. These were: 1) writing a fraudulent check for $1440; 2),3),4) signing three false reports in July, 1881, each of which indicated that the $3791 was "in transit" to San Antonio, when in fact he had embezzled the money; and 5) telling Colonel Shafter on 10 August that he had sent the funds to San Antonio, when in fact he had not.

The trial was quite complex, and after so long a period, there is much apparent conflict in the record which will probably never be resolved. For instance, while Lucy may have looked like Flipper's selfless protector by hiding the envelope filled with checks on her person, her motives become suspect when Shafter said in his testimony that she had tried to claim money found inside Flipper's trunk."[39]

Also, many witnesses at the trial commented on the number of civilians, mostly Mexicans, who seemed to be in and around Flipper's quarters when he was not there, and about the large amount of checks and currency that seemed to be almost carelessly strewn around his rooms.[40]

There was considerable suspicion expressed that some of these individuals, perhaps in collusion with Lucy, were thieves. But Flipper, who had learned Spanish at West Point and enjoyed using it with those who did not shun him because of his color, trusted his new friends even in financial affairs. He would testify: "I had no reason to question the honesty of any of the persons about my house as I had never missed anything that attracted my attention, and when the officers searched that trunk and failed to find the funds which I had put there three days before I was perfectly astounded, and could hardly believe the evidence of my own senses. As to where that money went and who took it, I am totally ignorant.[41]

Most of Flipper's own commissary bill, $1121.57, was for credit he had extended to enlisted men and civilian workers not normally allowed credit, and which was no doubt covered by the check for $1440 he had written and kept in his trunk while awaiting royalties from New York.[42] This check may also have covered amounts that had been pilfered from his quarters, but Flipper's records of debts from his loans and extensions of credit to others were too scanty to determine this point. When that amount is coupled with the $1400 in checks that were found on Lucy, a gap remains of another $900 that he should have had and that he did not realize he was missing at the time of his arrest. Flipper said he believed that this amount was in his trunk and was stolen from him by unknown persons. But whether it was stolen by Lucy, the Mexicans, or other officers such as Lieutenant Wilhelmi whom he did not trust is largely irrelevant. When the time came, Flipper was unable to produce the money. "It was simply a matter with himself and all there was of it, Lieut. Flipper, 10th Cavalry, did not pay his commissary bills to Lieut. Flipper, A.C.S.[Acting Commissary of Subsistence]. And might this discrepancy also be due just to Flipper's longstanding sloppiness in keeping records—lending more money to others than he realizzd, or spending more for himself than he realized? Readily understood -- compare credit card debt in modern times.

Given the time and place of the court martial, it has to be said that Captain Barber's defense was quite thorough. To a layman, some of the points he made may seem to be mostly "form over substance". But in the law, form can be all important. For instance, at the beginning of his summation, he quoted the specification of the first charge: "Lieutenant H.O. Flipper, 10th Cavalry, did embezzle, knowingly and willfully, misappropriate and misapply, public money of the United States, furnished and intended for the military service thereof, to wit: three thousand, seven hundred and ninety-one dollars and seventy seven cents ($3791.77), more or less, which money came into possession and was entrusted to him in the capacity of Acting Commissary of Subsistence at the post of Fort Davis, Texas."[43]

Barber thereupon made a sweeping plea of "not guilty". But before going to the specific merits of the case, he made an important point that looks, at first, like no more than an administrative error on the part of the prosecution team. But was it that simple? He argued: "Before entering upon the consideration of the circumstances on which the government bases this charge, I desire to direct your attention to an offense alleged in the specification which is not alleged in the 60th Article of War, under which it is laid, and that is "misapply". There is no such offense under the 60th Article of War...we are brought before you on an indictment under the 60th Article of War for something which is not an offense under that article." He then went on to point out that although the offense "misapply" may once have been in the 39th Article of War, it has been superseded by the 60th. [44]

Barber's main concern here was to eliminate the possibility that his client could be convicted of "constructive" (rather than "actual") embezzlement. If the .portion of the charge that read "misapply" had remained, rather than the newer and more specific language of the statute, "applies to his own use or benefit," then such a finding would have been possible. He then went into the specific legal definition of embezzlement, which meant an "intentional, wrongful, and wilful conversion of public money to his own use and benefit." [45]

The events of the preceding year were reviewed, and Barber showed that Flipper had never evidenced any intention to convert the money entrusted to him, nor any evidence of newly-acquired wealth, nor any secrecy or other suspect behavior. Once he had been arrested, he showed Flipper's willingness and ability to make good the amount lost through his own resources in short order as strong evidence of the lack of desire on his part to acquire such ill-gotten gains. Barber then showed that Flipper was expecting the amount of $2500 to arrive by check from his publishers in New York, and argued that Colonel Shafter's actions before and after the arrest showed that he was either shamefully forgetful, incompetent, and undependable, or was Flipper's active enemy, working to hurt him in any way possible.

Accepting that some money was missing, Barber showed that the bookkeeping practices and record maintenance procedures of the commissary service were fatally flawed before Flipper even arrived at Fort Davis, and that the missing funds were less his fault than that of the system itself. Then he went back to the definition of embezzlement, and showed that, if the funds had been stolen, Flipper was not even aware that had happened until after he had been arrested. The disappearance, Barber argued, was not caused by Flipper nor done with his knowledge, so that the element of intent was missing, and Flipper simply could not have kept the money and used it for his own purposes.[46]

Barber next addressed the second charge, that of "Conduct Unbecoming an Officer and a Gentleman." The first specification was that he lied to his commanding officer, telling him that the checks were in the mail to higher headquarters when he knew they were not. The second, third, and fourth were that he had submitted false reports to his commanding officer, when in fact he had kept the money and used it for his own purposes. Barber quickly disposed of these last three specifications: "All the testimony in this case is directed to the inaccuracy of one single entry of the funds in transit to the Chief Commissary of Subsistence, Department of Texas, and as there is nothing said of the other entries it must be presumed they are all true. It is necessary that every part of a specification should be covered in testimony and found by the court, and all that is not covered must be found for the accused, and in regard to the last averment of applying to his own use and benefit we feel as confident that you will not find Lieutenant Flipper guilty of embezzlement under this charge as under the first."

The fifth specification under this charge was that Flipper had presented a fraudulent check with the intent to deceive his commanding officer, Colonel Shafter. Barber took this specification on first: "It must have been known to the officer drawing the charges that the check had never been out of Mr. Flipper's hands, had never been uttered, published, or presented, had never been negotiated or used in any manner except as an exhibit.... The element which makes it fraudulent is uttering it, negotiating it, putting it in circulation. As nothing of the kind was done in this case, the averment that the check was fraudulent gives an entirely false coloring to the transaction and is a misuse of the term."[47]

Barber also argued that, on the only date the check was shown to Shafter, it was for an amount, $1440.43, that was much greater than any difference could have been on that date between the amount Flipper had on hand and the amount for which he was responsible. Therefore, the check was neither fraudulent nor meant to deceive Shafter.[48]

As to the first specification, Barber conceded that his client had not been truthful with Shafter, but he also showed that Flipper had been warned that Shafter would destroy him if he could, and that Flipper was desperate to stay out of trouble. Ever conscious of the fact that he was the only black officer in uniform and aware of the added attention that drew to his every act, Flipper made every effort possible to be seen as the sort of ideal officer who would meet the theoretical standards he had learned at West Point. Among other things, that included a man of high principles who would withstand any temptation to lower his standards for personal gain. But in the financial workings of the army's necessary logistical support, he desperately needed the guidance of a mentor, an older and wiser man who could help him along his path. Unfortunately, his race seems to have precluded such a relationship, and he had to tell Shafter small lies to buy time, in the hope that he could somehow acquire the money necessary, even if it was out of his own pocket, to make his promises good.

Barber then summed up this situation with typical lawyer's rhetoric: "Now, gentlemen, by what standard will you measure him? By that of your race or his? By his worth or his weakness? Will you judge him by his success through years of struggle and isolation or by an error to which he was moved by carelessness -- negligence, if you please -- and the dread of a harsh master? Is a man to be judged by his mistakes alone?...I have said that his people are on trial before you equally with himself, and this is so from the anomalous position that he occupies as their sole representative in the service, and the question is before you whether it is possible for a colored man to secure and hold a position as an officer of the army."[49]

Barber also spoke of the standards that had been set for the court martial charge of "Conduct Unbecoming an Officer and a Gentleman." In doing so, he quotes segments from Rollin A. Ives' 1879 treatise, *Military Law*, as they were used by various court-martials: "In one sense, every impropriety, every indecorum is unbecoming an officer, and equally so to a gentleman. But this is not the signification that the words have when employed in framing charges." In still another case that came up in that army it was held that "This article should only be used when the offense is such as to disgrace the offender to make him an unfit associate for officers and gentlemen, and to render his expulsion from the society of such, necessary to the preservation of the respect due to them as a class....An officer of the highest merit may, from indiscretion or thoughtlessness, or from momentary excitement, do an act which all right-minded persons would consider as highly unbecoming a gentleman, and yet, if it involved nothing dishonorable or morally wrong, he would not thereby forfeit his character as a gentleman."[50]

Barber then made specific reference to two recent court-martials for similar charges of "Conduct Unbecoming an Officer and a Gentleman" made under somewhat different circumstances. He recommended that, as they considered the charges made against Flipper, the court be guided by the construction of the Commanding General of the Army, General William T. Sherman, therein recorded.

The first case was that of a certain Lieutenant Hasson, found in the War Department's General Court-Martial Orders No.41 of 1879, who called one Doctor Steigers a liar in a conversation on an official subject. Hasson then struck him a "severe blow in the face, the Doctor having lost an arm in service and unable to defend himself." The court-martial found him guilty and sentenced him to be dismissed. In his review, General Sherman said: "The charge of violating the 613th Article of War should only be made when the conduct of the accused is such as to unfit him to be an associate of officers and gentlemen. It does not seem that Lieutenant Hasson's conduct was disgraceful to such an extent as that. Lieutenant Hasson's conduct was unjustifiable, especially in striking a one-armed man, and was clearly prejudicial to good order and military discipline, to which extent the court might have found him guilty, but it did not. Lieutenant Hasson will return to duty." [51]

The second case is that of Paymaster Reese, found in the War Department's General Court-Martial Orders No. 34 of 1872. The charges were embezzlement, conduct unbecoming an officer and a gentleman, and conduct prejudicial to good order and military discipline. There were fifteen specifications under embezzlement and seven under conduct unbecoming. The court acquitted on the first charge and substituted conduct prejudicial for conduct unbecoming on the second. Some of the review is as follows: "Here was an officer who for a period of about two years was, by his own admission, guilty of constant irregularities in his use of the public moneys [sic]; who repeatedly reported untrue balances to the Paymaster General.... Thus, by his gross carelessness and neglect of duty, the pecuniary obligations of the United States were publicly dishonored and the credit of the government so far compromised....The fact that the accused did not end up being a defaulter to the United States -- that at the last moment, to wit: on the day after that on which the order of his arrest was telegraphed from the War Department to Louisville, he caused the final overdrawing of his account at New York to be made good by a deposit in the Treasury of private moneys [sic] - doubtless influenced the court in the lenient view which they have taken of this case."[52].

The sentence of the court was "to be reprimanded in General Orders and to be suspended from rank and command for a period of four months." The order was published November 30, 1872, but the sentence as to suspension was remitted by President Ulysses S, Grant in General Orders No. 41 on December 7, 1872, and Paymaster Reese was restored to duty.[53]

Barber's closing argument to the court-martial is more than 70 double-spaced pages long. By the time of the twenty-first century, emotive or poetic words coming out of the mouths of lawyers have lost much of their sway in the court room. Even so, the last few sentences of Captain Barber's closing argument retain a power all their own: "May we not therefore ask this court to take into consideration the unequal battle my client has to wage, poor, naked, and practically alone, with scarcely an eye of sympathy or a word to cheer, against all the resources of zealous numbers, official testimony, official position, experience and skill, charged with all the ammunition which the government could furnish from Washington to Texas, and may we not trust that this court will throw around him the mantle of its charity, if any errors are found, giving him the benefit of every doubt, giving him the credit of that splendid record so eloquently expressed by Colonel Grierson of his regiment, giving him that consideration which his life of isolation justifies, giving him the advantage of that punishment he has already received, more severe than any it is in the power of this court to inflict, giving him the precedent established by the court in New York in the case of Paymaster Reese, so exactly parallel to this in its nature, but so much stronger in its features and – better than all else – giving him your confidence that the charity you extend to him so generously will be as generously redeemed by his future record in the service."[54]

It was the custom at the time that, if the defendant made a final statement, it would be the last the members of the court would hear before they retired to consider the case. If, however, the defense counsel made a final argument, then the judge advocate would be allowed to follow it with his own counter-argument, and that would be the last the court would hear. After Captain Barber finished, Captain Clous addressed the court. His argument was much shorter, and it emphasized simply that the money was missing and that Flipper had been responsible for it.

Clous gave great weight to the relationship between Flipper and his maid, Lucy. Clous reminded the court that only Flipper or Lucy had had access to the keys to the trunk, and argued that the two of them had been in collusion and that Flipper had either allowed her to withdraw the funds and somehow transfer them to a location from which he would later recover them, or had secretly taken the money himself with the purpose of applying it to his own use.[55]

The court-martial then ended for the public, and the members met in closed session to decide the case. The judgment handed down in January 1882 seems to have been predictable from the start: on charge one, not guilty; on charge two, guilty of all five specifications. The sentence prescribed was that Flipper "be dismissed from the service of the United States."[56]

An automatic review then occurred through the military chain of command all the way up to the President (the 106th Article of War at the time said that, in time of peace, no sentence of a court martial directing the dismissal of an officer shall be carried into execution before it has formally been confirmed by the President of the United States). The first reviewing officer was Brigadier General Christopher C. Augur, the Commander of the Department of Texas who had earlier directed Shafter to remove Flipper from the guardhouse. His review was quite harsh—even overturning the court's finding on the first charge: "In the foregoing case of 2d Lieutenant Henry O. Flipper, 10th Cavalry, the proceedings are approved. The findings of "Not Guilty" of the first charge & its specification are disapproved; the evidence seeming, in the opinion of the reviewing authority, to fully establish the allegations in the specification and "embezzlement" under the 60th Article of war. The findings upon the 2d charge, & the specifications under it, are approved.

The sentence is approved.

The Proceedings are respectfully forwarded for the action of the President."[57]

General Augur was not a lawyer, but he was clearly a stern man. The next reviewing officer was a lawyer, the man responsible to advise the Secretary of War on issues of law—the Secretary of War, by the way, being none other than Robert T. Lincoln, son of the man who had emancipated individuals such as Flipper. That was the Judge Advocate General of the Army, David G. Swaim. His report to the Secretary of War, the last comment before the President would review the case, was extremely detailed analysis of the testimony. He concluded by agreeing with the court martial's original finding of not guilty on the first charge (of embezzlement). On the second charge--"Conduct Unbecoming an Officer and a Gentleman"—he took up the argument made by Flipper that Colonel Shafter was out "to get him into trouble" and went on to say: "Subsequent developments convinced Lieut. Flipper that his information concerning the disposition of Shafter toward him was correct. It is believed that there is no case on record in which an officer was treated with such personal harshness and indignity upon the causes and grounds set forth as was Lieut. Flipper by Col. Shafter and the officer who searched his person and quarters taking his watch and ornaments from him; especially as they must have known all the facts at the time and well knew that there was no real grounds for such action...I would recommend that the sentence be confirmed but mitigated to a less degree of punishment.[58]

All that was left now was a final review by President.Chester A. Arthur. Given the recommendation for mitigation of punishment from Judge Advocate General Swaim, the senior lawyer in the army, it would not have been unreasonable to expect some leniency from the White House. But on 14 June, 1882, President Arthur signed a simple statement at the bottom of the cover letter forwarding the Flipper case to the White House from the War Department. It read: "The sentence in the foregoing case of Second Lieutenant Henry O. Flipper 10th Regiment of U.S. Cavalry, is hereby confirmed."[59]

Accordingly, Flipper was discharged from the army but remained in the Southwest. He worked as a civil and mining engineer, not only in the southwest United States but also, given his skill with the Spanish language, in Mexico as well. However, until the day he died in 1940, he adamantly insisted on his own innocence in the matters for which he had been court-martialed and driven from the army in disgrace.

As he recovered, Flipper began to establish a favorable professional reputation, such that he gained many friends and admirers. Eventually, he became close to governmental leaders and, through their agency, was able to have bills introduced in both Houses of Congress that would have restored him to the officer corps in the army.[60]

In the body of these bills, he proposed a number of new defenses to the charges made against him, most of them structural: That the attempt to force two new members on the court after it had been organized and accepted by Flipper seemed an effort to fix the composition of the court so as to guarantee conviction; that the merging of the functions of prosecuting and reviewing officer in one individual was prejudicial to Flipper; that three of the members of the court martial were assigned to the 1st Infantry and so worked for Col. Shafter, the man who preferred the charges; etc. These defenses seem almost technical, however, and short of a Presidential pardon, it is difficult to see how an appeals court might use them to overturn an earlier decision.

One of his new defenses, however, seems worthier than the others. That is the defense he makes to specifications 2), 3), and 4) of Charge 2: They all specify that certain funds he had falsely said were in transit had actually "been retained by him or applied to his own use or benefit." But that is simply a statement of the crime of embezzlement, a crime of which he had been found "not guilty" under the first charge, and so these three specifications of the second charge must also fall.[61]

Flipper's efforts to attain legislative overturning of a court martial verdict, however, were strongly opposed by the War Department, and all such bills died in Committee and were never brought to a vote on the floor of either the House of Representatives or the Senate. Flipper was relentless, and had bills introduced as late as 1922, but all failed. His efforts to have Congress officially clear his record and so return his good name to him unfortunately occurred at the same time that Jim Crow laws were springing up in the South to oppress blacks, while either anti-black sentiment or indifference to the second-class citizenship of blacks swept unimpeded through the nation.

In 1940, Flipper died a quiet death in Atlanta, but his cause did not die with him. In the early 1970s, Henry O. Flipper's nephew, Festus Flipper, and niece, Irsle F. King, submitted an appeal to the U.S. Army Board for Correction of Military Records. In their name, a Georgia schoolteacher, Ray MacColl, who had become interested in the case, prepared and submitted a 52- page brief. The brief drew heavily on Judge Advocate General Swaim's lengthy letter, and stated a number of technical errors or injustices in the composition of the court or in its proceedings, new defenses that had been brought up by Flipper in his attempt to get bills passed by Congress that he hoped would have restored him to military service.

The major problem with such criticisms of a trial that has already handed down judgment is that, even if granted by a court of review, they would only overturn the conviction, and the result is that the defendant would almost certainly be tried again on the same charges. After the passage of more than one hundred years, even if a court were to overturn an earlier decision on such grounds and no further trial were to be held because of the difficulties involved, the record would remain tainted, as the issues would not have been decided on the merits and disposed of once and for all.

This time the Flipper family had an ally inside the Pentagon. H. Minton Francis, USMA Class of 1944 and the eighth African American to graduate from West Point, was a deputy assistant secretary of defense. As such, he was able to help obtain serious consideration for the appeal. The Army Board for Correction of Military Records heard the appeal, delivering its decision on 17 November 1976. Early on, the Board stated an important limitation on its action:

"That the Attorney General of the United States (40 Opinions Attorney General 50) has held that the language of the statute which established the Board for Correction of Military or Naval Records cannot be construed as permitting the reopening of proceedings, findings, and judgments of courts-martial so as to disturb the conclusiveness of such proceedings; and that, however, such Boards might properly correct records as a matter in clemency or mitigation with reference to the sentence of such courts, including fines, forfeitures, reduction in grade, character of discharge, etcetera."[62]

The board made a number of statements about the harshness of the punishment meted out in 1882 and the record of service that Flipper had established both before and after his court-martial. The board recommended that the Army's official records be corrected to show that Flipper was separated from the Army with an honorable discharge on 30 June 1882.[63] On 13 December 1976, the assistant secretary of the Army for manpower and reserve affairs formally approved the findings of the board and directed that the Army records be changed. But even though the nature of his discharge was changed, Flipper's conviction of conduct unbecoming an officer remained on the books.

In 1989, Minton Francis, class of 1944 and one of the first African Americans to graduate from West Point in the 20th century, was at a meeting of the board of trustees for the West Point Association of Graduates, where he met one of the newest trustees, Federal Judge Eugene Sullivan, USMA Class of 1964. One of their conversation topics was a recent article about Flipper and the correction of his military records. Francis was surprised to learn that, in the eyes of the law, Flipper remained a convicted felon despite the successful action at the U.S. Army Board for the Correction of Military Records. In Sullivan's view, only a federal court could void the conviction.

The only other option was a pardon by the president. Francis asked Sullivan if he would help him clear Flipper's name. Though sharing the concerns of Francis, Sullivan could not practice law as a sitting judge, but he decided to read the historical records about the Flipper conviction.

Judge Sullivan asked his secretary, Barbara Burley, an African American, if she would volunteer to obtain the Flipper court records on microfiche from the National Archives. Burley was eager to assist in clearing the name of an American officer of great moral courage whose skin happened to be black. Once she had secured the relevant records, Sullivan was surprised to find that the stack of papers was easily 10 inches high. He asked his wife, Lis, to read through the documents and mark the relevant sections of the legal proceedings, including her perception of bias or unfair treatment in the court-martial. A major undertaking, this was an important weeding of handwritten records that were often difficult to read.

Once this step was completed, Sullivan reviewed the distilled records and concluded that there were numerous instances of injustice in the trial. These included the illegal confinement of Flipper before the trial, which was a violation of the 65th Article of War in effect at the time; command influence by Colonel Shafter; attempted jury tampering, again by Colonel Shafter; improper review of the conviction by the Prosecutor, Captain Clous; inconsistent verdicts; lack of sufficient evidence to support the verdict; prosecutorial misconduct in charging the wrong offense; and other prejudicial factors. But now Judge Sullivan had a problem: even though he could see that justice had not been done in this case, he could take no action to remedy the injustice. In fact, he had decided that if the case ever came to his court, he would recuse himself because of prior knowledge.

Judge Sullivan's frustration with forced inaction seemed to be resolved when he and I had lunch together. I am also both a graduate of West Point and a lawyer, and Judge Sullivan was delighted to find someone who might help him in working to clear Flipper's name. I took his stack of historical records home and read them almost immediately. I agreed with Judge Sullivan's conclusions that injustices had occurred, and decided to make this issue a key part of my dissertation. But as a lawyer admitted to practice in federal courts, I also wanted to take legal action in Flipper's behalf.

My dissertation covered the factual and legal history of the Flipper case, to include the relevant official records and the specific instances of seeming injustice, both in the trial and on appeal. After completing the dissertation, I started drafting a legal brief intended for filing in federal court in an attempt to overturn Flipper's conviction. But as I worked, it became increasingly clear that I would be opposed in court by the U.S. government on many grounds — legal, political, administrative, bureaucratic, etc. This could be a long, difficult, and expensive fight, and it was just too risky and too important for me to pursue by myself. What I really needed was a large Washington D.C. law firm that had the resources and the will to accomplish this most worthy goal. Jeffrey H. Smith, also a West Pointer, was a partner in such a large D.C. law firm. In fact, Jeff and I were in the same class both at West Point and at the University of Michigan Law School, and he was eager to help. Thereafter, Smith and his partners and associates explored the possible legal avenues for redress. Eventually, they decided that the best and most practical route would be a presidential pardon. It took more than five years, but their effort was eventually successful. Bill Clinton pardoned Henry Flipper on 19 February 1999, the first posthumous pardon ever granted by a U.S. president.

The initiative resulting in a presidential pardon for Flipper was a team effort: West Point graduates who worked to right a wrong done to another graduate long ago, not because he was a graduate, nor because he was African American, but because he was a victimized young Army officer who deserved better. In the words of Epictitus, the Roman Stoic philosopher, they extended themselves in Flipper's behalf simply because they wanted to "do the right thing".

Endnotes: Chapter 6

1. Flipper, *Colored Cadet*, pp 247-8.
2. Flipper, *Negro Frontiersman*,(El Paso, 1963), pp.14-16.
3. Ibid, pp.15-17.
4. Ibid, p.18.
5. Ibid, pp 2-3
6. *The Army and Navy Journal*, 17 (11 October 1879), p. 176., and Theodore D Harris, *Henry Ossian Flipper: The First Negro Graduate of West Point.* University of Minnesota Unpublished Ph.D. Dissertation in History, 1971, p. 139
7. Flipper, *Negro Frontiersman,* p.19
8. "Court Martial Proceedings of Henry 0. Flipper", File QQ2952, Record Group 153. The record of these proceedings, 744 pages in length, is found in the National Archives. pp.300-304 of that record. Hereafter, these Court Martial records will be referred to as "CMR"
9. CMR., pp.53-54.
10. CMR, pp.301-304.

11 Flipper, *Negro Frontiersman*, p.32.
12 Flipper's possessions in his quarters were inventoried on 18 August 1881, after his arrest, and the list appears as Exhibit 83, p. 724, CMR
13 CMR, pp. 477-484.
14 The testimony of Sergeant Ross contains much detail about how the commissary was run, at pages 391-412, CMR.
15 CMR, p.54
16 CMR, exhibit number 109, p.745
17 CMR, pp. 535-540.
18 CMR, p.575.
19 CMR, p.538
20 CMR, p[. 503
21 U.S. House of Representatives, 55th Congress, 2nd Session, Committee on Military Affairs: In the Matter of the Court-Martial of Henry Ossian Flipper, p. 12.
22 CMR, pp 122, 129
23 CMR, p.444.
24 CMR., p. 504
25 CMR, p. 522
26 CMR, p. 508
27 CMR, pp. 655-658 and pp. 503-505, wherein Flipper stated that the weekly verification of funds did not occur from 28 May through 8 July, corroborated by the weekly statements not having been signed by Shafter or his designee. On pp.507 and 508, the Judge Advocate called a witness to testify that the books had been checked on June 4, but after a conference, the court refused to allow such testimony.
28 CMR, p. 649.
29 CMR, pp.306-307.
30 CMR, p.506.
31 CMR, p.193
32 CMR, pp.67-68
33 CMR pp. 68-73
34 CMR, pp. 75-77.
35 CMR, p.50.
36 CMR, p.51.
37 CMR, pp.25-60.
38 CMR, pp.150-152.
39 CMR, p.121.
40 CMR, pp. 284-290.
41 CMR, p.504.
42 CMR, pp.410-411.

43 CMR, pp.508-509.
44 CMR, pp.511-512
45 CMR, p. 515
46 CMR, pp. 523-553
47 CMR, p. 557.
48 CMR, pp. 57, 524-526, 565-568
49 CMR, pp.577-578.
50 CMR, pp.560-561.
51 CMR, p.561.
52 CMR, pp.561-562
53 CMR, p.562
54 CMR, pp.583-584.
55 CMR, pp.593-94.
56 CMR, p.605.
57 CMR, p.606.
58 Letter to the Honorable Robert T. Lincoln, Secretary of War, from Judge Advocate General David G. Swaim, dated 3 March, 1882; copied on unnumbered pages located in Record of Proceedings of Henry O. Flipper's trial by General Court Martial, File QQ 2952, Record Group 153, National Archives.
59 CMR, p.607.
60 E.g., 55th Congress, 2d Session, H.R. 9849, April 13, 1898; 56th Congress, 1st Session, S. 1260, December 11, 1899.
61 CMR, p.607
62 Proceedings, In The Case of Henry O. Flipper (Deceased), U.S. Army Board for Correction of Military Records, 17 November 1976, 6.
63 Ibid., 7.

J. H. Alexander – Ohio

CHAPTER 7

John Hanks Alexander

After Whittaker left in 1882, the next African-American to be admitted to West Point was John H. Alexander, who was admitted on 1 July 1883. On 2 July, the day after his swearing in, a long and interesting article about Alexander's future days at West Point appeared on the front page of the *New York Times*. The article was little more than the verbatim comments of a member of the Second Class (which means he had just completed his Third Class, or Sophomore, year) at West Point. This interview was taken on 30 June 1883, in Washington (presumably the District of Columbia, though this is not noted in the byline) where the cadet was then on leave.[1]

A summary of the thrust of the interview appears in the article's opening paragraph: "The future of the latest colored cadet appointed to the West Point Military Academy is not destined to be much happier than that of the operatic policeman if the views of a Second Class man, who has conversed about the matter, are correct. Mr. Alexander is sure to be ignored socially, and will succeed, if he does succeed, with such credit to his strength of purpose and superior manliness as will entitle him to be regarded as one of the heroes of the century." [2]

Clearly, if his success will justify his being recognized "as one of the heroes of the century," that which awaits him must be quite intimidating. But those are the words of the reporter, and in good American newspaper tradition, it would not be unusual if they were somewhat of an inflation of what the cadet interviewed in Washington actually said. In fact, the cadet's statement in the first paragraph of the interview is not quite so bone chilling as the reporter would have us believe: "I believe there will be no commotion among the cadets over the admission of Mr. Alexander, and I believe he will suffer no special inconvenience on account of his race. On the contrary, I believe he will receive special consideration on that account, both from the officers and cadets: not because he will be preferred, but because of a feeling that to practice on Mr. Alexander any of the usual fun practiced on plebes by cadets, or to give him the ordinary punishment daily administered by tactical and cadet officers, would be misinterpreted and give rise to a cry that Mr. Alexander was an object of persecution on account of his color."

The reporter then asked: "Will the cadets associate with Mr. Alexander?" And the cadet replied: "I don't believe any cadet will associate with him - that is, in a social way - not even members of his own class. This will not, however, interfere with opportunities to maintain his standing in his class and in his corps. There is abroad a mistaken notion about social enjoyments at West Point. There is very little opportunity for such enjoyment, and for the Fourth, or 'Plebe' Class, there is none outside of class association."[3]

The cadet interviewed here is never named, and is referred to only as "a Second Class man" and "the gentleman." But that anonymity does not necessarily imply falsehood. Indeed, his comments are not out of keeping with the feelings of cadets during that period. And the above-quoted section, which is probably no more than one sixth of the body of the interview, betrays the blinders then worn by West Point cadets.

The cadet predicts that there will be no commotion among cadets about Alexander's admission, that care will be taken to avoid the false impression that race affects his treatment at West Point, and that members of the public may be misled so far as to adopt his (Alexander's) "erroneous belief about persecution on account of race" - and this before Alexander has even reported to West Point. But the telling section comes next: we are told that, first, no other cadets, even members of his own class, will associate with Alexander, and second, that there is very little chance for social enjoyment at West Point, and for members of the Fourth Class, there is "none outside of class association."

So we are told that there is and will be no racial prejudice expressed against Alexander, and almost in the same mouthful, that he will be excluded from any social association with anyone, including his class, and that the only chance for social enjoyment comes through social association - from which Alexander is excluded because of his race. It seems clear that racial prejudice was so widespread and even taken-for-granted among white cadets at West

Point, that even when it appeared in blatant form, as here, it was often not even recognized. But of course, as was seen earlier in this work that was also true in 1883 throughout most of the nation.

John Hanks Alexander was born in Helena, Arkansas, in 1864, the child of two parents who were described as "mulattoes" in the census. His childhood and life were to be most unusual for one born in the deep south to parents who had been slaves. His father, James Milo Alexander, was born in Virginia in 1815. In the 1830s, his owner, Lawson Henderson Alexander, moved to a plantation in St. Francis County, Arkansas, where James spent the next decade. His mother, Fannie Miller, was also Virginia-born, but moved to St. Francis County with her master, Colonel Abijah Allen. Fannie was soon owned by Lawson Alexander, for whom she became a house servant. In short order, she married James Milo Alexander, the coach-man of her new owner. In 1844, their first son, named Milo after his father, was born. But two years before that childbirth, Lawson Alexander had died, and this event meant a profound change in the lives of James and Fannie. They then fell under the permissive control of two of Lawson Alexander's children: Mark, who became an important attorney in Helena, and his sister Nancy, who married a prominent physician in the same river town. Under their watchful eye, both James and Fannie learned to read and write, and lived with privileges that set them far apart from the masses of slaves in Arkansas who spent their lives working in the cotton fields.[4]

In the late 1840s, James Alexander had moved to Helena, where he opened a barber shop, which he advertised in local newspapers. He was probably the property of Mark and Nancy Alexander, but they gave him free rein to work and earn money. He had left his wife and children in St. Francis County, but he began to buy his freedom and theirs before the start of the Civil War. When John Hanks Alexander was born on January 6, 1864, it was to free parents.[5]

During and after the Civil War, James Alexander became active and successful in the dry goods and grocery trade, but a broken levee in 1867 seriously damaged his store, and wiped him out as a businessman. Ever resilient, however, he built on his good business reputation and became active in politics as a Republican. Before long, he was justice of the peace, school trustee, and member of a grand jury in Phillips County. Then he died suddenly in 1871, at the age of 56. Fannie, industrious and resourceful, worked hard as a maid and a cook so that her children could get educated.

They attended Oberlin College, the University of Michigan, and West Point, and at one time or another, four of her children were teachers.[6]

John graduated first in his class from the all-black high school in Helena, then went to Ohio and enrolled at Oberlin College, where he studied for two years. In order to pay for his education, he worked as a waiter at the Weddell House, the leading hotel in Cleveland, where he established lasting relationships with many prominent members of the African-American community. One of these would become his life-long friend: John P. Green, a black attorney and politician, with whom he later corresponded, and these letters today provide much of the sparse information we have about Alexander.[7]

Having read about Flipper and other black cadets at West Point, Alexander decided to apply for an appointment from Congressman George Geddes of Mansfield, Ohio. He received a strong recommendation from his Oberlin professor of Greek, William G. Frost, who said that his performance in that classical course had been uniformly excellent: "He is," said Frost, "a young man of pleasing address, good character, and very rare ability as a student. He enjoys the esteem of his teachers and will always have their best wishes for his true success."

Alexander was one of only two young men who passed the initial examination given in Elyria, Ohio, the other being William Waites, the son of Ohio's Chief Justice. Although Alexander had done better on the academic test, it was discovered that he had a condition described as being "pigeon-breasted." Waite was therefore given the principal appointment to West Point, and Alexander received the first alternate - meaning that, should Waite somehow fail to pass the admission tests at West Point, then Alexander would next be examined for the same appointment. When Waites failed the academic admission test at West Point, Alexander excelled and was admitted as a cadet with the class of 1887.[8]

The admission of black cadets at West Point was an issue of some note to newspapers, and several reporters were standing by to see what would happen. But as it turned out, there was not much of a story to report. *The New York Times* reporter (quoted above) noted that after Alexander took the West Point admissions tests, his appearance in a hotel lobby while awaiting the results was largely ignored, because no one seemed to want to associate with him. The reporter continued: "I happened to sit next to him at dinner in the West Point Hotel today, and was glad to be able, by talking freely with him, to give him a social status in the dining-room that most of the guests did not seem inclined to accord him. I found him a very clever and intelligent young man, fully equal in appearance and manners to any of the candidates I have met and much superior to many of them....Alexander is a rather dark mulatto, with a bright, intelligent face...He is cheerful as a lark, and it is impossible to talk with him for ten minutes without wishing him the best of good luck.[9]

From the shade of his skin reported in the last article, it would seem that, unlike Whittaker, there would be no possibility that other cadets might mistake Alexander's race. Also, the reporter notes an engaging and apparently optimistic personality in Alexander that may explain the fact that he seems to have been more accepted by white cadets than were those blacks who preceded him.

The black press was naturally interested in Alexander's arrival and admission to West Point. According to the *People's Advocate* of Washington, D.C., Alexander's success was important evidence to black youth of the value of hard work and perseverance. "Mr. Alexander is...possessed of the qualifications necessary to force his way even against the opposition of the cod-fish aristocracy at West Point. He possesses as much manhood to the square inch as any white man at the Academy and will doubtless make many friends there. Still the colored man shows a disposition to come to the front and all the prejudice and opposition of the closed corporation of the Academy will be powerless to prevent his ultimate equality."[10]

The Cleveland Gazette also took great pride in what was an undeniable major accomplishment for a young black man: "It was learned at the War Department that Alexander, the Ohio colored cadet who was admitted to the Academy upon passing the examination after the white boy whose alternate he was had failed to pass, occupies a very different position in the Academy from that of Flipper and Whittaker. Alexander is treated as an equal by the boys of his class in their work and their play. No difference is made between him and any other boy by his comrades. All this without constraint on the part of the authorities of the Academy, and in the most natural way possible. The instructors think well of him....John H, Alexander is progressing finely at West Point."[11]

This is certainly a positive report, dated September 7, 1883, about race relations at West Point. It must be diluted somewhat, however, by the apparent source of the news and its timing. The article is datelined "Washington" and opens with information acquired from the War Department. It seems doubtful, therefore, that a black newspaper in Ohio sent its own reporter to a small military post isolated fifty miles north of New York City. Rather, it seems likely they just relied on a news release from the War Department, which would not have wanted to spread anything but good stories about race relations at West Point. But by September 7, 1883, Alexander, had only been there less than three months and academic classes had just begun. Still, there are other stories about Alexander's social acceptance by other white cadets, in marked contrast to the closed social doors that met other black cadets, so perhaps there is more than a grain of truth in this *Cleveland Gazette* story.

Alexander was obviously intelligent, but he was also familiar with the experiences of Smith, Flipper, Whittaker, and the other African-Americans who had received appointments. His goal was graduation, and he worked hard to achieve that end. After his first semester, the *Cleveland Gazette* was buoyant: "He is making a better record than any colored cadet ever admitted....Adjutant Eli Hoyle speaks of him as a splendid scholar. Getting along finely, and says that while the officers of the post in no way interfere or indicate to the white cadets the course they must pursue towards the colored cadet, they had noticed with feelings of satisfaction that the colored cadet so deported himself as to win the esteem of many of the corps."[12]

Alexander's grades at West Point are of interest. At the end of his Fourth Class year, in the General Order of Merit (which included grades as well as military deportment), he stood number 16 out of 100 cadets. In English, he was ranked number 4, in French number 7, and in Mathematics number 13. Unfortunately, he had received 144 demerits for the year, and was ranked number 42 in discipline. And this relatively low ranking - although it was still in the top half - dragged his class rank out of the top 10 to number 16.

Thereafter, he gradually slipped downward in class rank as the numbers in his class shrank: Although 122 had enrolled in his class, only 64 were to graduate. He graduated from West Point on 11 June 1887, ranked number 32 out of 64 cadets in the overall Order of General Merit over four years.[13] He was ranked in the middle both in academics and in conduct, and so far as can be seen more than a century later, he was an unremarkable, completely normal cadet. He got in trouble only occasionally and in modest ways. One of the few notations that he stepped seriously out of line during his cadet career was when he was punished for kicking his horse during Cavalry drill (his alleged immediate outcry that the horse had kicked him first was to no avail).[14] Unfortunately for the historian in later years, because he was never the center of major scandals resulting in courts martial, as were both Smith and Whittaker, few revealing records of him survive in the West Point Archives. And unlike Flipper, he never seems to have written about any of his experiences.

While Alexander was at West Point, four other black cadets were admitted, but only one of them, Charles Young was to graduate. Young was admitted in June 1884, while the others came after him. William Trent Andrews from South Carolina and William Achilles Hare were sworn in June 14, 1885. Hare's complexion was so light that he was presumed to be white by other cadets—that is, he apparently "passed" for being white. Appointed from Ohio, Hare was also a friend of John P. Green, and corresponded with him. In one early letter, Hare provides a unique view of West Point in the summer of 1885: "There is one colored cadet among the new ones by the name of Andrews. He is quite a nice young man and is liked by the more intelligent class. He attends strictly to his own business, is rather conservative in conversation, never pushing himself forward in any manner and all told is a very gentlemanly young man.... There is considerable color prejudice among the new cadets and it exists among the Southerners especially. They are continually murmuring when they have to walk beside Andrews and some of them say that they will not do it. I had quite a time with a Southerner by the name of Hill. None of the boys know that I am colored and I can easily find out what their sentiments are. This Hill, several others and myself were in the shoe-black room and we were talking about several of the boys, when Hill said that they should not allow niggers in the academy and that they were beasts. I became angry at this and I told him that they should not permit a rebel to enter this institution. He also became angry, and we were about to have trouble, and would have had it not been for the want of time. I am glad to say that he failed and Andrews passed. This instance is one of many but I think that it should be stopped. They dare not make any demonstrations of their being prejudiced but one can see it in every action they take regarding color."[15]

Both Hare and Andrews, unfortunately, were found deficient academically after one semester, Andrews in Math, Hare in Math, English, and Discipline. Both men left West Point in January 1886. Henry Wilson Holloway from South Carolina was admitted on 1 September 1886, but he, too, was found deficient in Math after only one semester and left the Academy in January 1887. Holloway was the last African-American admitted to West Point in the nineteenth century.[16]

It is difficult to measure the isolation Alexander endured as a cadet. The experiences of black cadets who had preceded him, as well as the *New York Times* interview with a white cadet that appears at the beginning of this chapter, seemed to indicate that he would be subjected to the same social exclusion. No doubt this is what he was accorded by many white cadets. But there are too many other indications to be ignored that he was accepted by at least some of his peers. Unfortunately, even the few of his letters that survive give less than a clear picture.

A letter from February of his sophomore year is illustrative: "You can not realize to what extent I have been shut off from all refining influences (social) and how utterly West Point is isolated from the rest of the world. Were it not for changes in the climate and stream of visitors that come here it would seem that I had spent the last two years in the confines of the highest and most secluded peaks of the Himalayan mountains. Just to think of a person going two years without speaking to a woman! Of course, most other cadets have friends visiting them and enjoy social advantages at hops and with the families of officers, which advantages are closed to me. I hope, however, that the positive wholesome influences at work will render this a very slight offset. Taking these facts into consideration you will probably not be amazed when I tell you that no imprisoned criminal ever looked forward to the day of his release with more pleasure and happy anticipation than I do to my coming summer vacation furlough."[17]

Clearly, West Point was no picnic, but except for his reference to the fact that "hops and the families of officers" were closed to him, this letter could have been written by a lonely white cadet, for the isolation of the Academy affected all who there resided, not just black cadets. But the white situation was dramatically different from that faced by black cadets – of being constantly and totally ostracized and shunned, and often harassed when even noticed at all.

Alexander was careful to keep his dissatisfactions and loneliness to himself and a few close friends. To the rest of the world, he presented a demeanor of utter equanimity with his situation at West Point, and it is clear that he knew what he was doing, for he had carefully studied the experiences of black cadets who had preceded him at West Point: He wanted only to succeed.

Despite his refusal to complain about racist outrages he had to endure, he was ever aware of the wrongs being done to other blacks in his native south. For instance, in March 1886, in Carrollton, Mississippi, a confrontation between a white man, J.M. Liddell, and a black man, Ed Brown, led to a shootout on the streets, after which several blacks were arrested. During the trial, an organized group of armed white men took over the court house and killed a dozen black men, including Ed Brown, who had been accused of being "impudent" to whites.[18]

This event, known as the Carrolton Massacre, truly aroused Alexander, as he revealed in a letter to John Green: "My soul was deeply stirred to the very depths by the massacre of colored people in Carrollton, Miss.... Because a colored man and his friends have the courage to stand up and resist and resent the impertinence of an insolent, overbearing white man, the latter's friends club together and at the trial open fire and coldly murder this colored man with 10 or 12 of his friends and wound several others.... I honor this colored man Ed Brown as Irishmen do Robert Emmett as all men do Spartacus. A man that can thus stand up for his right - his manhood - when low public sentiment all conspire to make him a cringing, cowardly, servile brute, I say such a man is more than a man, he is a hero....We are not living in the middle ages, and we are citizens of a country where all men are free and equal. Moral suasion is a good thing, but a little courageous manhood is now in great demand.... So long as we submit, of course, they will think that we have no rights that white men are bound to respect."[19]

To be sure that his mother, Fannie, could attend his graduation, Alexander had been saving money to buy her a round-trip railroad ticket from Helena to West Point. When the moment came, she was there, tall and stately and as proud as she had ever been, an ex-slave who was witnessing her son's triumphant graduation from West Point.[20]

It was said by some that he received more applause than any of his classmates when he stepped forward and received his diploma from General Philip Sheridan. As a cadet, he had distinguished himself as a very good rider,[21] and upon graduation, Alexander was commissioned a Second Lieutenant in the 9th Cavalry, one of two all-black Cavalry Regiments then stationed on the western frontier.

After graduation, he was interviewed by the *Cleveland Gazette*:

> "Did you find any prejudice on the part of the students against your color?"
> "Yes, a little, but it soon wore off...."
> "How did you enjoy it?"
> "It isn't a life to be enjoyed altogether. It's one long, incessant strain, without any letup. But I think I got as much fun out of it as the next man." [22]

After graduation, Fannie returned to Arkansas, and John Hanks Alexander left for two months of leave. Thereafter, he proceeded to his first assignment with the 9th Cavalry at Fort Robinson, in Nebraska. These black cavalrymen, along with their sister all-black 10th Cavalry Regiment, were the "Buffalo Soldiers", and they had earned a certain distinction pacifying the west and protecting settlers. Just as in Flipper's day, however, it was only the enlisted ranks that were "all black"; the officers in command, with the exception first of Flipper (now gone more than five years), and next of Alexander, were all white. By this time Alexander, as he was no doubt aware, was the only African-American serving in a command post in the entire United States Army. No matter how he might have played down the responsibility he now carried, others were very attentive to his every step. A black editor in Kansas said: "It remains to be shown that he will carry into life the renown with which he graduated. It is one thing to do well in school, and it is another to prove adequate to the task devolving upon us after we have graduated. The country, especially the Negroes, will look to see the mark that Cadet Alexander will make in life, the result of which will raise or lower the estimate of the Negro population as he is a success or a failure."[23]

Alexander stayed at Fort Robinson until March 1888, then he and his troops were transferred to Fort Washakie, Wyoming. A few months later, in June, he was moved to Fort Du Chesne, Utah, where he was to remain for three years. During a leave in 1890, he visited his family in Arkansas, then traveled to Charlotte, North Carolina, to inspect a black militia unit, the Charlotte Light Infantry. After another leave, he was sent back to Fort Robinson. Duty on the high plains on horseback was hard and wearing, and Alexander "remained an inconspicuous second lieutenant" for six years.[24]

At the time, the army's officer ranks were still bloated with Civil War veterans, and this was not an unusual time to await promotion to first lieutenant. At long last, in October 1893, he was examined for promotion to First Lieutenant. He told his old friend Jack Green that he hoped to be promoted in about six months.[25] Then, out of the blue, he received orders to report to Wilberforce University in Xenia, Ohio, on January 6, 1894, a black school, where he would be the professor of military science and tactics. The school's president, W.S. Scarborough, had been able to convince the War Department to make this assignment, and no one was more pleased than Alexander himself to be returning to Ohio.

Instead, tragedy struck. On March 26, 1894, while in a barber's chair in Springfield, Ohio, Alexander complained of a severe headache, then collapsed and died of what was later believed to have been a heart attack. There was great mourning in the black community and among many whites as well.

One black editor in Kansas City spoke for a much larger body of grieving Americans: "The Negroes of the United States can ill afford to lose a man like Lieutenant John Alexander. His sudden death is a shock to us, and we sincerely mourn his untimely end. A young man of unusual brilliancy, with a long and useful career before him, to be cut down just at the beginning of life, as it were, is a sad blow to the whole race."[26]

ENDNOTES: Chapter 7

1. At that time, the only leave a cadet received during four years was two months in the summer after his Third Class year. When the furlough class returned, most came on a boat from New York City, and when they unloaded, they all came storming up the hill from the dock onto the Plain in a mass, looking like nothing so much as a herd of cows. From that time until the present day, all members of the Second Class at West Point are uniformly known as "Cows."
2. *New York Times*, July 2, 1883, p.1
3. Ibid.
4. Willard B. Gatewood Jr, "John Hanks Alexander of Arkansas: Second Black Graduate of West Point", *Arkansas Historical Quarterly*, 1983, Vol. 41 (1982), pp. 103-128.
5. IIbid,pp.105,109.
6. Ibid, pp. 108-112.
7. Ibid, p.116; these letters form part of the Green Papers in the Western Reserve Historical Society, Cleveland, Ohio.
8. Ibid, pp. 112-117
9. *New York Times,* June 13, 1883
10. *The Peoples Advocate.* Washington DC. July 17, 1883
11. *Cleveland Gazette,* Washington, D.C., September 15, 1883.
12. *Cleveland Gazette,* January 19, 1884.
13. All of Alexander's academic records are in the US Military Academy Archives, West Point, N.Y.
14. *Cleveland Gazette* July 2, 1887.
15. W.A. Hare to John P. Green, June 28, 1885, in John Patterson Green, Ms 3379, Microfilm Edition, Western Reserve Historical Society, Cleveland, Ohio (hereafter "Green Papers")
16. Cadet Records, U.S. Military Academy Achives
17. John H. Alexander to John P. Green, February 8, 1885, Green Papers.
18. *New York Daily Tribune*, March 18, 1886; *New York Freeman*, April 3, 10, 17, 1886.
19. John H. Alexander to John P. Green, March 27, 1886. Green Papers
20. *New York Freeman,* June 18, 1887; *Cleveland Gazette,* June 18, 1887.

21 *Cleveland Gazette*, June 18, 1887.
22 Ibid, July 2, 1887
23 Nicodemus (Kansas) *Western Cyclone*, Jul 1, 1887.
24 Gatewood, pp.120-125; John M. Carroll, ed., *The Black Experience in the American West* (New York, 1971), p.266.
25 John H. Alexander to John P. Green, November 17, 1893, Green Papers.
26 *Kansas City American Citizen*, March 30, 1894.

CHAPTER 8

Charles Young

Charles Young entered West Point one year after Alexander, and was his constant companion, although he would repeat one year and thus would spend his last two years at West Point as the only black cadet in residence. He would be the last African-American to graduate from West Point in the nineteenth century, and it would be another 47 years before the next African-American, Benjamin O. Davis, Jr., the son of the first African-American general officer in the army, Brigadier General Benjamin 0. Davis, Sr., would graduate from West Point in 1936. Two other African-Americans would be admitted earlier in the twentieth century - John Byron Alexander in 1918 and Alonzo Souleigh Parham in 1929 - but both were found deficient (Alexander in Conduct, Parham in Math) after only one semester and left before they had really even gotten started.[1]

Young was born in a log cabin in Mayslick, Mason County, Kentucky, close to the Ohio River, on 12 March 1864. His parents had been slaves and his father may have served as a private in the Union Army. In 1872, his family moved across the river to nearby Ripley, Ohio, where Charles grew to manhood. He was a bright student, graduating from high school at the age of 16. He spent several years teaching high school, all the while preparing to enter a Jesuit college by studying Greek and Latin under a Catholic priest. Then he took a competitive examination for an appointment to West Point and, like Alexander before him, won the "first alternate" appointment. When the young man who held the "principal" appointment failed the admission test, Charles Young passed easily and entered the ranks of the corps of cadets on June 15, 1884.[2]

As mentioned earlier, he roomed with John Alexander, and for the next three years, they were each other's best friends. It appears unlikely, as discussed in the previous chapter, that Alexander was completely "silenced" by all white cadets. Young, however, was less popular, and the curtain of silence probably did fall around him, especially after Alexander graduated in 1887. Although black Cadets Andrews, Hare, and Holloway were to enter before Alexander graduated, they were all there for only one semester, and Alexander and Young were together both before the others arrived and after they left. Socially, then, Young was placed in the same predicament as other black cadets before him: He was left strictly alone socially by white cadets.

Young was a natural linguist and musician. By the time he was forty, he had easy use of Latin and Greek, and he was fluent in French, Spanish, and Portuguese,[3] he played the piano and the violin, and delighted in writing music for both instruments,. However, none of these attainments would help him in mathematics, which he failed at the end of his first year. His other grades at the end of his first year were certainly respectable: out of a class of 82 cadets, he was ranked number 25 in French and number 32 in English, but because of his failure in mathematics, he was "turned back" on 17 June, 1885, and had to repeat his plebe year.[4]

This time, out of a class of 75 cadets, he ended up number 32 in math, number 8 in English and number 8 in French. He was ranked number 46 in discipline, and his overall Order of General Merit was number 34. During his Third Class year, he dropped to number 50 out of a class of 56 cadets, and during his Second Class year, he was number 46 out of a class of 51.

His First Class year saw more academic difficulties, for he was found deficient in Engineering in June. After five years of lonely exasperation, this had to be a particularly crushing blow. But the dogged dedication of Young had been recognized, and a special program was established whereby he might still win his diploma and his commission. He stayed on at West Point for two months of special instruction to try to make up for his failure to the satisfaction of the all-powerful Academic Board. Fortunately for him, his instructor of Engineering during his First Class year, Lieutenant George Goethals,[5] volunteered to stay and work with him. Given his grit and determination, he passed his final test on August 31, 1889, and received his diploma and his commission as a Second Lieutenant two months after the rest of his class.[6]

What had Young's social life really been like at West Point? Had reason begun to set in? Did he not have white cadet friends with whom he could openly associate? Did he even get the occasional friendly smile or wink? Or was he still walled off by all? The official eulogy for Young was written by Major General Charles Rhodes, Young's classmate at West Point. It appeared in the June 12th, 1922, Annual Report of the Association of Graduates of the U.S, Military Academy, less than six months after his death. And while it is predictable that one will read only of shared fond memories in eulogies, it would appear that General Rhodes was overly kind to West Point and to those who were cadets during Young's days at the Academy.

One section of this eulogy indicates this: "It cannot be said that during his first years at the Academy Young was a popular cadet. Left much to himself, he had few opportunities to exhibit likable traits of character, and he made few friends. But it must be said that he gained ground each year at West Point, and in the fifth and last year, after having patiently shown for the past four years a dog-like perseverance in the face of many natural handicaps, his own class began to acknowledge and respect his finer traits of character; while a spirit of fair play induced many cadets of character and standing in the corps to treat Young with the kindness and consideration which had long been his due."[7]

That sounds as though in 1889 or so, at long last, white cadets had finally begun to treat black cadets as their peers - which, legally, they were. This idea is reinforced by a letter Rhodes wrote on his graduation day: June 9, 1889: "All is over and at length has come the bridal day, of beauty and of strength... Our colored classmate, Charles Young, whom we esteem highly for his patient perseverance in the face of discouraging conditions which have attended his cadetship for five years, did poorly in both Engineering and Ordnance; and was given a special, written examination in each subject.... We are hoping that Young will get through; it would be a terrible disappointment to lose the coveted diploma, after five years of intensive work."[8]

Written at the time of the class graduation, that sounds as though Young had been befriended by many white cadets, including Rhodes. But was the "esteem" Rhodes speaks of openly expressed to Young, or simply harbored as a private feeling? How did Young feel about his social relations with his white classmates as a cadet?

Fortunately, a letter he wrote from Monrovia, Liberia, on 26 July 1915 to Delamere Skerrett, a classmate who also happened to be a fellow Ohioan, can shed some light on the issue. After some preliminary remarks about what he is doing in Liberia, he thanks Skerrett for "remembering me at the Class dinner last year at the Point" and then he spoke from his heart: " You know for me the Academy has, even to this day, heart-aches in spite of the many advantages I derived there. The sole bright things that come to my heart are the friendship and sympathy from men like you, Bethel, Webster, McGlachlin, Harrison, Lambdin, Langhorne, Barnum, and Bandholtz. Yes, I must mention the disinterested help of Col. W.B. Gordon and General Goethals - I can never forget them; and have tried to pass onto others the kindness of you all, both in America, the Philippines, the West Indies and Africa. So you see you can not always tell the wide reaching influence of a word of cheer to even a black man. God knows how many white ones I have helped because you all helped me. Simply trying to pay the interest on the debt of gratitude I owe you, that's all. The world is better and only worth living in because it has its Skerretts, Bethels, Goethals, Gordons, Barnums, Haans and Langhornes with the others of that stripe. May they live long." [9]

That letter puts a different light on matters. And, indeed, when he talks of "friendship" that was shown by white cadets, given the tenor of the times, I expect that his comment about a "word of cheer to even a black man" was probably about the extent of what he got. Still, years later, one can feel deeply grateful for just a sip of water in the middle of a desert.

Young's first assignment after graduation was to the 10th Cavalry, the all-black regiment. Then, within a few months, he was shifted to the other all-black regiment, the 9th Cavalry, at Fort Robinson, where he got his first real taste of the frontier for a year. In September 1890, his unit was reassigned to Fort Duchesne, Utah, some 170 miles from Salt Lake City and far from civilization. There, Young was truly isolated, for white officers were largely unbending in their unwillingness to socialize with blacks, and officers simply did not fraternize with enlisted men. An efficiency report from that period states that he was "liked and respected but very much alone socially."[10]

After more than four years of difficult life in the high mountains and plains of the west, Young was called back to service in his home state of Ohio. In 1894, after John Alexander's untimely death at Wilberforce University, Young was named by the War Department to succeed him as Commandant and Professor of Military Science and Tactics. In addition to his official duties, he also taught the upper classes in French and in higher Mathematics. He was very much a hero to his students, and even the president and faculty seem to have been awed by him: A smart, articulate, black West Point graduate who had spent years of grueling service on the frontier and had come back to teach black youth.[11]

In 1897, Young was promoted to first lieutenant, and in 1898, given command of the 9th Ohio Volunteer (Colored) Infantry, with temporary rank of Major of Volunteers. Although he wanted to lead his troops to Cuba and join in the fight, he never got there, passing instead through various training stations at Camp Alger, Virginia, at Camp Meade, Pennsylvania, and in Summerville, South Carolina. Young was mustered out of the Volunteers on January 28, 1899, and returned to Fort DuChesne, Utah, as a first lieutenant.

Not content simply to go through his paces, one of the memorable things he did there was to organize and instruct a brass band and other musical ensembles, which put life into the step of men stationed at a lonely outpost. He also promoted singing in ranks while marching, and one of his enlisted men, Benjamin O. Davis, Sr. (who would later win a commission and rise to become the first black general officer in the U.S. Army) retained memories many decades later of the strong impression this had on the men. In 1900, Young noticed Davis and encouraged him in his application for a commission, and even gave him special instruction in mathematics; he would write him a strong letter of recommendation, describing Davis as "temperate, polite, intelligent, trustworthy, and faithful to the duties of his office."[12] Young was promoted to Captain on 2 February 1901, and in April left for duty in the Philippines in command of "I" Troop, 9th Cavalry.[13] Davis would be commissioned a 2nd Lieutenant that same year and so join Young as one of the only two African-American officers in the U.S. Army.[14]

The 9th Cavalry was sent to the Philippine Islands to put down the insurrection that had emerged in the aftermath of the Spanish American War. This was Young's opportunity to lead his men in combat, an opportunity he had long relished. But no doubt the romantic aura soon wore off, for he and his men were engaged in some 18 months of heavy guerrilla fighting in Samar, Blanca Aurora, Duranga, Tobacco, Rosana, and San Joaquin. In February 1902 they helped force the surrender of Lukban, chief of the Visayan insurgents, but the campaign was bloody, and one newspaper reported that "Samar was a place of dark and bloody fame. There more died by far than had fallen in the Spanish American War from all the armies involved."[15]

In October 1902, Young and his men returned from the Philippines and were stationed in the Presidio of San Francisco. In May 1903, he received orders to serve as the superintendent of the Sequoia National Park for one summer season. After a 16 day ride, he reported there with his "I" Troop, a place where he would set new standards. The Sequoia National Park had only been in existence for thirteen years, but it was still just a section of the wilds in California's Sierra Nevada mountains that was difficult to visit. The development and management of the Park was the responsibility of the Army,[16] but because of a lack of funding by Congress, almost nothing had been done when Young arrived. The major requirement was for a wagon trail to the Giant Forest, where the largest trees in the world were to be found. The Army had begun work on a road in 1900, but after three summers,[17] only five miles of it had been finished.[18]

The main responsibility Young and his men faced, he learned upon arrival, was extension of the wagon road. With the same energy and dogged commitment he had always shown, Young set his men to work. By mid-August, wagons were using the newly finished section of the road to enter the mountain-top forest for the first time. "I" Troop pressed on, and within weeks had extended the road to the base of Moro Rock. During the "summer" work period of 1903, Young and his men had completed as much road as had been constructed over the preceding three "summer" work periods. And an inspecting Officer reported that Young's troop was "undoubtedly the best instructed of any on duty in the parks."[19]

Back in San Francisco in 1904, Young married Ada Mills of Xenia, Ohio. In May, they went to Port au Prince, Haiti, where Young had been appointed the U.S. military attaché. This was the first time an African-American had been appointed military attaché to any country. But his assignment was broad, in that he was also directed to acquire as much intelligence information on Haiti (which United States forces would later occupy) as possible. Consequently, he traveled widely on horseback, sending maps and traverses and detailed reports on all aspects of Haitian life to Washington. He was also somehow able to put together a French-English-Creole dictionary, and to write *The Military Morale of Nations and Races*, which was later published in Kansas City in 1912.[20]

While he was serving in Haiti, Young also extended a helping hand to Benjamin O. Davis, Sr., now a first lieutenant. Davis was assigned to fill the role of commandant and professor of military science and tactics back at Wilberforce University, and Young rented him his furnished home there for $24 per month. This was the exact amount Davis received each month as a housing allowance. It was a comfortable house, with an attached stable, and Davis and his young wife and baby daughter were comfortable there for several years.[21]

Young returned to Washington in 1907, where he served with the intelligence department of the Army's general staff from May 1907 until

June 1908. He then left with his wife and young son for a second tour of duty in the Philippines, where he was stationed at Camp McGrath, first as a troop commander, then as the commander of the 3rd Squadron, 9th Cavalry. He returned after a year, and commanded the 2nd Squadron, 9th Cavalry at Fort D.A. Russell, Wyoming, where he stayed through the last days of 1911. From December 31, 1911, through March 30, 1912, he worked in the office of the chief of staff of the U.S. Army in Washington, D.C.[22]

While in the nation's capital, he spent long periods with Benjamin 0. Davis, Sr., just returned from several years as military attaché in Monrovia, Liberia, which post Young was scheduled to assume. Davis briefed him extensively on the difficult situation that awaited him: Davis had observed the Liberian army and militia and found that they were not only inept, but that the government could not control them. Davis recommended both to Washington and to the Liberian government that the Liberian army be put under the command of five Americans: three noncommissioned officers and two officers, with himself acting as a lieutenant colonel and chief of staff, and John Greene, the other African-American who had received a commission from the ranks, acting as a major and quartermaster. This proposal was not accepted, but when the Liberian government later asked Davis if he would accept an appointment to run their army, he refused to give up his U.S. commission. He did, however, pass the question back to Washington, asking if they would detail him to Liberia to perform such a service. This request was ultimately denied on constitutional grounds.

Thus, Young would not actually have command of Liberian forces, but when he went to Liberia, it was with the understanding that his presence in that country "just to give advice" would be a total waste of time for both sides. Therefore, while he could not be formally accorded authority, it was agreed by both sides that his "advice" would be closely followed in all cases.[23] Once he arrived in Monrovia, in addition to his duties as attaché in the Embassy, Young also worked with the general receiver of customs and was centrally involved in the organization and training of both the Liberian Army and the constabulary. On August 28th, 1912, Young was promoted to major in the regular army, and thereby became the first African-American to reach that rank.[24]

While serving in Liberia, Major Young stayed as active and involved as ever. In addition to the complete reorganization of the army and the constabulary, Young also mounted military expeditions as the need arose. For instance, he led one column of troops to rescue one of his subordinate

American officers who had been attacked by cannibals deep in the jungle, in the process receiving a gunshot wound in the right arm. He also suffered from a prolonged case of blackwater fever, which is an often fatal infection of the urinary tract brought on by malaria.[25] But he stayed committed to his duty and even got started on his old habit of road building, as we can see from the opening paragraph of a letter he wrote on 26 July 1915: "It is a long hike to you from a camp in the jungle of Liberia where I'm trying on nothing save a rice bag (to give the soldiers "chop") to make a road from the Capital Monrovia, through the 'big bush" to the hinterland. I find that the coast has done all it can for the country and that if it is ever going to be developed and saved to my people we must get to the native man in the interior and on the hinterland. 1. The Frontier Force reorganized. 2. A map of the country made for them. 3. I set myself this final task prior to yielding myself to the Manchu law next summer."[26]

The "Manchu law" was an Army regulation in force before World War II which forbade Officers in the regular army from serving more than three consecutive years away from troops—that is, in administrative assignments. When Young came back from Liberia, he was awarded the Spingarn Medal by Massachusetts Governor Samuel McCall before 3,000 people on February 22, 1916, at ceremonies in Boston. This gold medal was awarded annually to the man or woman of African descent and American citizenship who had made the highest achievement during the year in any field of elevated or honorable human endeavor.

His next military assignment was to command the 2nd Squadron of the 10th Cavalry. This was one of the first units to go after Pancho Villa in Mexico, and they were relentless in their pursuit. When one Major Tompkins and his men were ambushed near Parral in an affair that, according to the *New York Times*, "nearly brought the American and Mexican governments to the verge of hostilities," it was Young and his squadron who rode to their rescue.[27] Young was promoted to lieutenant colonel "in the field" on July 1, 1916, and did not relinquish command until March 12, 1917. John Pershing was the commander of the Punitive Expedition into Mexico, and he would become the commander of the American Expeditionary Force that would fight in Europe during World War I. At the end of the foray into Mexico, Pershing reviewed the performance of his subordinate commanders, and submitted a list of those who should be promoted to brigadier general and command a brigade in the event of mobilization for war. Young was on the list for promotion to general.[28]

But there were complications and traps waiting. The first one was sprung in June, 1917, while the American Expeditionary Force was mobilizing. At a routine promotion board to colonel, Young sailed through, but at the required medical board, he was stopped and told that, because of "high blood pressure," he was not healthy enough to remain on active duty. Further tests at Letterman Hospital determined that he had sustained levels of blood pressure in the 230/150 range, and chest radiography showed "an enormously enlarged heart, hypertrophy of the left ventricle." But Young was also suffering from nephritis (Bright's disease), which would eventually kill him in 1922, and this had been noted in his medical records as early as 1911. This malady was never made public, and the Army only announced his high blood pressure as the medical cause of his retirement. And so the African-American rising star not only failed to make general, he was left out of the fight in France. [29]

On June 22, 1917, Young was promoted one grade to full colonel and retired for "disability contracted in Line of Duty.[30] But Colonel Young was not ready to retire. The only public explanation the Army had given for Young's retirement had been his high blood pressure. In order to refute that, in June, 1918, he mounted a horse in his hometown of Xenia, Ohio and rode all the way to ashington, D.C. He took several weeks to travel some 500 miles, and his trip was widely publicized in the African-American community as proof of his good health. Upon arrival, he met with the secretary of war, and eventually was called back to active service, but not until November 6, 1918 - five days before the Armistice.[31]

Soon after Young returned to service as a colonel, Liberia asked that he be sent back there to continue helping them build their nation.[32] Young accepted this posting, but before he left, he spoke to the congregation of St. Mark's A.M.E. Church in New York City on December 14, 1918. Asked why he opposed the erection of a war memorial to Negro soldiers who died in the World War, he responded: "If Congress wants to do anything for the black soldiers who died in the service of their country, let the Congress of the United States come clean and give them the thing for which they fought - liberty!"[33]

Colonel Young left for Liberia in January, 1919, but little more was heard of him beyond official reports, until January 8, 1922, when he died of nephritis while on an intelligence mission in Lagos, Nigeria. His body was initially buried with full military honors by the British in Lagos, but in 1923, at the request of his family, his body was returned to the United States, and on 1 June, was escorted through Washington, D.C. by a troop of the 3rd Cavalry, a regiment of the segregated army that was made up exclusively of white soldiers. Then, in the company of a large crowd of mourners, Colonel Charles Young was formally laid to rest. He would be the last West Point cadet openly acknowledged to be African-American who would graduate from West Point until Benjamin O. Davis did so in the class of 1936. [34]

ENDNOTES: Chapter 8

1. "Black Cadets Admitted to USMA," Archives of the U.S. Military Academy, West Point.
2. *Cullum Biographical Register*, Cullum No. 3330, Association of Graduates, U.S. Military Academy, West Point, N.Y.; New York Sun, July 8, 1912; *Washington Post*, May 20, 1929.
3. E.H.Lawson, "One Out of the Twelve Million," *Washington Post*, May 26, 1929.
4. Young's academic record is preserved in the U.S. Military Academy Archives, West Point
5. Goethals would later gain fame as the engineer responsible for the completion of the Panama Canal.
6. Annual Report, U.S.M.A. Association of Graduates, June 12, 1922, p.153
7. Ibid, p.152.
8. Extracted from *Intimate Letters of a West Point Cadet* by Charles D. Rhodes; Rare Book Room, U.S. Military Academy Library, West Point, N.Y.
9. Special Collections, U.S. M. A. Archives, West Point
10. Nancy G. Heinl, "Colonel Charles Young: Pointman", *Army Magazine*, March, 1977.
11. Dr.W.S. Scarborough (Formerly President of Wilberforce University),"A Tribute to Colonel Charles Young", pp.7-8, Special Collections, U.S.M.A, Archives, West Point.
12. Marvin E. Fletcher, America's First Black General, (Lawrence, KS, 1989), pp.22-25
13. *Cullum's Biographical Register*, Cullum No, 3330, U.S.M.A., West Point
14. Benjamin O. Davis, Jr. *American*. (Washington DC), 1992.
15. "One out of the Twelve Million," *Washington Post*, May 26, 1929. This last statement about casualties may or may not be a slight exaggeration: the one volume *American Military History* published in 1988 by the U.S. Army's Center of Military History has a lengthy section on the Spanish-American war, which ends on page 339 as follows: ""Operations in the winter of 1899-1900 cleared insurrectionist elements from the Manila region and permanently secured important lines of communications in Central Luzon and the Visayas. In May, Otis, believing the insurrection virtually over, requested his own relief, and General MacArthur replaced him. Events proved Otis mistaken, for the Army had to continue in the field for many more months, dealing with sporadic but

persistent resistance in numerous small engagements. The guerrilla war was bitter and costly, resulting in more casualties for the Army than in the entire preceding fifteen months of extensive military operations. In early 1902, unrest among the Moros in Mindanao and the Sulu Archipelago intensified, and was by no means really settled when President Theodore Roosevelt announced on July 4 the formal end of the Philippine Insurrection."

16 The Army had assumed the responsibility to patrol and administer all National Parks, a duty it retained until the establishment of the National Park Service in 1916
17 A "summer" work period for the Army in the Parks depended on the climate, and Young was at Sequoia from May until November.
18 Wm. C. Tweed, " Black Army Captain in Charge During Sequoia National Park's Early Years," pamphlet published by Sequoia and Kings Canyon National Park, no date, U.S.M.A. Archives
19 Ibid
20 Heinl, p. 174
21 Fletcher, pp. 36-37
22 *Cullum Biographical Register*, Cullum No. 3330., U.S.M.A., West Point
23 Fletcher, *First Black General,* pp.40-44. 24 New York Sun, August 30, 1912.
24 *New York Sun*, August 30, 1912/
25 *Army-Navy Journal,* August 11, 1917.
26 Letter from Young to Skerrett, Special Collections, U.S.M.A. Library, West Point, N.Y.
27 *New York Times,* January 13, 1922
28 Heinl, p. 175.
29 Ibid.
30 *Cullum's Biographical Register*, Cullum No. 3330.
31 Heinl. Op. Cit.
32 *Army-Navy Journal*, December 13, 1919.
33 Ibid, December 20, 1919
34 Heinl, p.176

CHAPTER 9

A Mixed Record

We have followed the stories of the twelve African-Americans who gained admission to West Point during the years 1870 to 1886, a period of relative enlightenment. But with the end of Reconstruction the negative attitudes toward blacks held by whites in the United States now held sway and so once again even that path to progress was closed. After Charles Young, the next blacks were admitted in 1918 and 1929, but each lasted only one semester. Nearly half a century passed between Young's graduation and that of the next black who would graduate. During that time, the racial attitudes of whites toward blacks were so bad that no young black had much real hope of attending West Point.

Despite later negative changes in racial attitudes that were often embodied in law, as we have seen, those of the post-Civil War period held by white Americans were still quite bad. Even so, this look at a brief period has allowed us to see painfully slow but significant improvement in the conditions black cadets faced. But before going through the improvements, I would like to quote a letter from the Editor of a black newspaper, the *Cleveland Gazette*, written to the Editor of the *New York Post*, which the *Post* printed on July 26, 1929, under the bold, all capital caption:

WE DOUBT THIS PROPHECY.

It reads as follows:

To the Editor:

> Sir - There are four Afro-American Regiments in the United States Army. Lieutenants Henry O. Flipper, John Alexander, Charles Young, Afro-Americans, were all officers in those regiments, two of which are infantry and two cavalry. Alexander and Young were Ohioans, and all three were graduates of West Point, the United States Military Academy. Alexander and Young are dead, and Flipper, a fine civil engineer, is in South America. Colonel Davis and Colonel Greene, the two Afro-Americans in the United States Army, rose from the ranks and have had commands in these four regiments: Ninth and Tenth Cavalry and Twenty-Fourth and Twenty-Fifth Infantry, United States Army. Colonel Greene is retiring, and Colonel B.O. Davis, a resident of this city, is on furlough en route to Europe with his family.
>
> I thought possibly the foregoing might interest you. Afro-American officers can and will eventually command white troops of the United States Army just as General Dodds, the eminent Afro-Frenchman, and other so-called "negroes" commanded French (white) troops.
>
> Harry C. Smith
> Editor, *The Cleveland Gazette*

The point of the letter and its prophecy is that, by the time the letter was printed, the prophecy had, at least technically, come true many times over-- thus completely exposing the *Post*'s editorial ignorance and bias. But we will look at that in due course. Let us first look at some of the progress won by African-Americans at West Point.

James Smith broke the ice, but in addition to being the first African-American cadet, his unwillingness to swallow his pride meant that he was never given a fair chance to complete the program. He fell by the wayside for what were purportedly academic reasons alone, but in a somewhat different social environment, with the support rather than the opposition of his classmates, he might well have been able to succeed.

Henry Flipper learned from Smith, kept his feelings to himself, endured, and graduated. However, within a few short years, he was run out of the Army on what were little more than trumped up charges for minor offenses from which a white officer would have walked away unscathed.

Johnson Whittaker was struck in the face by another cadet soon after his arrival. While Smith had often endured blows with no recourse, Whittaker simply reported the offender, who was thrown out of the Academy for his offense. Only through Congressional appeals was he able to return, but he lost a year, and when he came back, he had to repeat that academic year in which he had attacked Whittaker. Another first was the way in which Whittaker, having failed a course in physics during his junior year, was allowed to simply stay in school and repeat the second semester of third class math to help him, after which he repeated the first semester of second class physics and did much better. The attack on his person remains a mystery. But whether he was attacked by three unknown men or staged the attack himself, it is clear that the pressures he endured trying to stay afloat academically in an environment as strongly racist as was West Point in 1880 made his life extremely difficult.

John Alexander sailed through West Point, and there is considerable evidence that he was not as completely walled off socially as had been those black cadets who preceded him. He graduated, and went off to serve in the Army, but unfortunately died unexpectedly of natural causes some six years later.

And finally, Charles Young took African-American West Pointers to new heights of success. After having been forced to repeat his first year because of academic failure, he failed the final exam in engineering just before he was to have graduated in June 1889, five years after he first arrived. But the academy made a special arrangement, whereby he stayed at West Point and was tutored through the summer, took another final exam in August, passed, and received his diploma. This option of staying on to repeat failed academic work despite having earlier been allowed to repeat an entire year for the same reason was a liberty that had been denied to both James Smith and Johnson Whittaker. He later became the first black major, lieutenant colonel, and colonel in the U.S. Army.

Long before the *New York Post* scoffingly printed the prediction by the Editor of an African-American newspaper in Cleveland that American black officers would one day command white soldiers, Colonel Young had done so repeatedly, in at least a technical sense, in a still-segregated army. He was the first African-American regular army officer to do so, although he did not command white units. Rather, the whites under his command were white officers, the white troop commanders and platoon leaders who served under him when he commanded the black enlisted men of the 2nd and 3rd Squadrons of the 9th Cavalry in the Philippines and in Wyoming. And when he commanded the 10th Cavalry Regiment for a year while chasing Pancho Villa through Mexico, his subordinates included white squadron (battalion) commanders as well as troop commanders and platoon leaders.

Admittedly, Young's command of a large body of black troops in the 9th and 10th Cavalry, the officers of whom were white, is significantly different from the command of a military unit in which both officers and men are white. But only a few years earlier, white officers such as these had ostracized 2nd Lieutenant Henry O. Flipper, and now they were commanded by another black West Point graduate. The symbolism as well as the reality are both there and significant.

The importance of this narration of the experiences of young black men at West Point is to be found in the steady progress they attained. Their successes were not handed to them, but rather were won by them, often in the face of the greatest overt opposition and naked hostility. But they each held to their course, believing that the officers of the U.S. Army who made up the staff and faculty at West Point would, at a bare minimum, uphold their individual rights and require such of the white cadets who made up the corps of cadets.

While the officer corps at West Point did require that the individual rights of black cadets were protected, they drew the line at social intervention, and repeatedly refused to attempt to interfere with the social lines drawn by cadets. Unfortunately, the tradition of allowing cadets to include or exclude other cadets socially was already well established when the first black cadets were admitted. This "cutting" of some cadets by the majority, which completely excluded them socially and left them friendless and far from home, often drove them to leave West Point. Even so, the officers charged with the administration of the academy were unwilling to change established traditions by interfering in what they deemed to be social issues, issues that were, finally, left to the individual consciences of each cadet.

The power of peer pressure at that time and place cannot be overemphasized. The specific warning associated with the particular social exclusion of West Point was understood by all: if a cadet spoke to another cadet who had been "cut," then that cadet, too, would be "cut" and thus condemned to the cold solitude that meant for the remainder of his time at West Point. When this is added to the tenor of the times and the low social esteem accorded to blacks by most whites of all classes throughout the country, then the strongly racist attitudes harbored by almost all new white cadets as they arrived at West Point can be better understood. Even the son of ardent abolitionists who might seek to interact socially with his black fellow cadets understood that to do so would be at great peril to his own social life. Unfortunately, there were precious few hands of friendship extended to African-American cadets by their white colleagues during the nineteenth century.

After the Civil War, the officers who taught and otherwise administered the corps of cadets at West Point were part of that victorious United States Army which had suppressed by force the efforts of the Confederate States to break up the Union. In the process, of course, the Civil War had led to the abolition of slavery. Most Union officers in that war, often because of their own firsthand experiences, had acquired more sympathetic and tolerant attitudes toward the freedmen, and these attitudes endured and affected the staff and faculty at West Point.

However, great care must be taken here. The fact that officers might have changed their attitudes toward blacks who had only recently been slaves, such that they might feel, say, that blacks should be allowed to vote, does not mean that these same officers would willingly invite blacks into their homes as their social guests or, indeed, that they would expect that any sort of social intercourse might flourish between black and white cadets. In fact, this divide between legal rights extended to freed slaves and social liberties denied them was to long haunt West Point, just as it did most of American society.

From its earliest days, the purpose of the United States Military Academy at West Point has always been the training and education of young officers who will, after graduation, serve the nation by leading the soldiers of its army. In time of war, many West Pointers risk their lives, bleed, and die. But in order to inspire young men to willingly take such risks, more is required than personal competence with weapons or knowledge of the strategy and tactics of past wars. While effective instruction in the military arts is central, the development of strong character traits committed to a vision greater than self is more important still. No matter how low-born, all admitted to West Point become by that act "Black Knights of the Hudson" and are taught in both subtle and blatant ways that, as the heirs of the Knights of the Round Table, they must always hold themselves above venal or corporal temptation, that there is no higher calling than a call to serve one's country under arms in time of war, that their lives will be committed, from the moment they don cadet gray, to selfless service to the American people.

Since long before the Civil War, West Point has stood proudly on a rock of high idealism, a rock that is said to divert the flow of the river of temptation for personal gain or fame. Cadets are young, and in the protected environment that West Point establishes within its walls, they are very quickly caught up in that closed society of the Long Gray Line which they fought to join. With acceptance of and by that society comes a sense of high responsibility, of honor, of mission, of filling a role in the nation's life that far outstrips any insignificant personality. Once this communion of fraternal bond and noblesse oblige has been established, the rest of the idealistic message of selfless service unto death is more easily absorbed and retained.

In nearly two hundred fifty years of existence, the United States has fought twelve major wars in as many generations. West Point's institutional history teaches that, every twenty or thirty years, a set of young West Point graduates will find themselves with their lives on the line. And when the blood-chilling ripple of gun fire and the nose-bite of cordite announce to a young army officer his own mortality and that of his men, his leaders do not want him to abandon his responsibilities and seek only to stay alive at whatever cost to others. Rather, they would prefer him to think selflessly of how he can, as the ancient Greek Stoic philosopher Epictitus advised, do the right thing: "What is the most desired outcome of this moment for our nation's leaders who sent me and the men under my command into harm's way?" Romantic and forced as it may sound, there genuinely is a regularly recurring time when our nation needs young leaders who are filled with the transcendent moral commitment and indomitable physical courage that will cause them to offer their lives pro patria.

West Point really tries, in the tradition of Socrates, to teach its cadets virtue - let the rational power rule, followed by the passions and the will - and virtue is needed by those who will risk their lives for the welfare of others. But if the virtuous conduct learned there allows a priori presumptions of racial superiority and exclusivity, then it is flawed. Cadets at West Point resisted the presence of African-Americans for almost a century after they first arrived. More ethical problems arose at the end of the twentieth century, as cadets resisted the admission of other minorities distinguished by gender or sexual preference.[1]

The staff and faculty when the first black cadets arrived toward the end of the nineteenth century were all West Point graduates themselves and so supposedly prepared to show great moral courage when moments of pressure arose. Given these enduring institutional claims of high ideals and morality, how would we assess the performance of these men?

In the most favorable light possible, their performance was rather disappointing. It is clear that many black cadets might have gained immeasurably from prudent application to their situations of the measured judgment of older, wiser officers then serving at West Point. These men might have alleviated some of the unfortunate strain under which black cadets were forced to live simply by inviting them into their homes socially. Unfortunately, such assistance was seldom made available.

The most that can be said about the performance of the staff and faculty, then, is that, in light of circumstances as they saw them, most white officers charged with command and administration of the U.S. Military Academy at West Point apparently tried to see that the specific tenets of the law were upheld as regarded the rights and freedoms of black cadets. Unfortunately, their perceptions of the law specifically ignored social acceptance of blacks by white cadets, which they held to be inviolable rights retained by individual cadets and with which they refused to interfere.

The nearly thirty years that elapsed from 1889 until 1918 saw no black cadets at West Point. But given that cadets obtained their appointments to West Point from Members of Congress or the President, this gap is really attributable to national attitudes, reflected by elected government officials. During the 1890s, as Jim Crow laws erupted across the South, black Americans saw many of their newly won freedoms restricted or eliminated. This included appointments to West Point, and once again, the corps of cadets was lily-white.

Two African-American cadets lasted one semester each in 1918 and 1929 before Benjamin O. Davis Jr. arrived. He graduated in 1936, the first African-American graduate in the twentieth century, became a widely-renowned fighter pilot in World War II, eventually rose to three-star rank in the Air Force, and later served as Mayor of Cleveland, Ohio.

After Davis, blacks began to win appointments more regularly, and by the end of WWII, each class entering West Point generally included one or more black cadets. As the civil rights of blacks became the focus of national attention in the 1960s and '70s, their numbers at other American colleges began to swell. West Point also began to admit more blacks, and over the last few decades of the 20th century, and into the 21st century, 4 to 7 percent of each new class at West Point has been made up of African-American cadets.

To these specific individuals, the history of their predecessors is obviously all important. Unless someone had come before them to break down the walls that excluded them and others of their race, they could not be what they are today: West Point cadets preparing to serve their country.

The history of African-American West Point cadets in the nineteenth century, then, is more than just an unusual collection of anecdotes that are, by themselves, of little more than passing interest. Rather, they are the sequential narration of young men facing the most intimidating of trials. Most were unable to endure the heat and intensity, .and fell by the wayside. But three earned diplomas in the nineteenth century, and gradually, their successes built into a legacy that has spawned African-American acceptance and professional success in the Army all the way to the top.

For African-American cadets in the nineteenth century, there was no easy path to success. Their diplomas, rather, were won under the most difficult of circumstances, usually in the teeth of the most belligerent opposition and open hostility from many of their contemporaries. But by staying the course and setting the precedent, these few valiant Americans laid the groundwork for the success of later generations in the more open military of today, where race has almost disappeared and merit has become the key to success.

ENDNOTES: Chapter 9

1   Female cadets reported strong gender-based hostility during the first years that they were admitted to West Point and although that may have abated, they still have somewhat limited access to all aspects of the army after graduation.

BIBLIOGRAPHY

National Archives

M1002 - Selected Documents Relating to Blacks Nominated for Appointment to the Military Academy During the 19th century 1870-1887.

The records reproduced in this microfilm publication are from

- Records of the Adjutant general's Office, 1780s-1917, Record group 94.
- Records of the Secretary of War, Record Group 107.
- Records of the Office of the
- Judge Advocate General (Army) Record Group 153.

On the 21 rolls of film in this publication are reproduced documents relating to 27 blacks nominated for appointment to the U.S. Military Academy during the years 1870-1887, apparently the only blacks nominated during the 19th century. The Documents include nomination and appointment papers, other correspondence, reports of examinations, consolidated weekly reports of class grades and conduct rolls, orders, and court martial case files. No documents are here reproduced that relate to the military careers of nominees following their graduation from the Academy.

Material relating to the military career of Henry O. Flipper after he left West Point is not included in M1002 above, but rather is found under the heading "Court Martial Proceedings of Henry o. Flipper", File 002952, Record Group 153, National Archives, Washington, DC.

U.S.. Military Academy Archives, West Point, NY.

In addition to much of the material contained in the National Archives, the West Point archives retain copies of various official and unofficial correspondence relating to the institution itself as well as to cadets both generally and specifically; academic records, disciplinary matters, and various other internal issues (e.g., "An Address Delivered by Maj. Gen. J.M. Schofield to the Corps of Cadets, United States Military Academy, West Point, N.Y., Monday, August 11, 1879."). In addition, the "Special Collections" branch of the U.S. Military Academy holds copies of correspondence to, from, and among cadets, of their memoirs, and various other writings.

Books

Ambrose, Stephen A. *Duty, Honor, Country: A History of West Point.* Baltimore: Johns Hopkins Press, 1966.

Ayers, Edward L. *The Promise of the New South.* New York: Oxford University Press, 1992.

Basler, Roy A., ed. *The Collected Works of Abraham Lincoln.* New Brunswick, NJ: Rutgers University Press, 1953.

Bender, Thomas, ed. *The Antislavery Debate.* Berkeley, CA: University of California Press, 1992.

Berlin, Ira, ed. *The Black Military Experience.* New York, Cambridge University Press, 1983.

Billingsley, Andrew. *Climbing Jacob's Ladder.* New York: Simon & Schuster, 1992.

Black, Henry Campbell. *Black's Law Dictionary.* Revised Fourth Edition, St. Paul, MN: West Publishing Company, 1968.

Black, Lowell D. and Sara H. Black. *An Officer and a Gentleman; the Military Career of Lieutenant Henry Flipper.* Dayton, OH: Lora Company, 1985.

Blassingame, John W.. *The Slave Community.* New York: Oxford University Press,. 1972.·

Bolster, W. Jeffrey. *Black Jacks*. Cambridge, MA: Harvard: University Press, 1997.

Bowen, David W. *Andrew Johnson and the Negro*. Knoxville, TN: The University of Tennessee Press, 1989.

Broderick, Francis L. *W.E,B, DuBois*. Stanford, CA: Stanford University Press, 1959.

Burns, James M. *The Vinyard of Liberty*. New York: Knopf, 1982.

Carroll, John M., ed. *The Black Military Experience in the American West*. New York:. Liveright, 1971.

Coffman, Edward M. *The Old Army, A Portrait of the American Army in Peacetime, 1784-1898*. New York: Oxford University Press, 1986.

Connell, Evans. *Son of the Morning Star*. San Francisco: North Point Press, 1984.

Cox, Lawanda. *Lincoln and Black Freedom*. Columbia, S.C.: University of South Carolina Press, 1981.

Crackel. Theodore J. *Mr. Jefferson's Army*. New York: New York University Press, 1987

David, Jay, ed. *Growing Up Black*. New York: Avon Books, 1992.

Davis, Benjamin O., Jr. *American: An Autobiography*. Washington, DC: Smithsonian Institution Press, 1991.

Douglass, Frederick. *My Bondage and My Freedom*. New York: Miller, Orton & Mulligan, 1855.

Downey, Fairfax. *Indian Fighting Army*. New York: Charles Scribner's Sons, 1944.

Doberman, Martin, ed. *The Antislavery Vanguard.* Princeton, NJ: Princeton University Press, 1965.

DuBois, W.E.B. *Black Reconstruction in America.* New York: Atheneum, 1935, 1992.

Dupuy, Ernest R. *Men of West Point: The First 150 Years of the United states Military Academy.* New York: William Sloane Associates, 1951

_____*Where They Have Trod.* New York: Frederick A. Stokes & Co., 1940

Elkins, Stanley M. *Slavery.* New York: Grosset & Dunlap, 1963.

Elkins, Stanley M. and Eric McKittrick. *The Age of Federalism.* New York: Oxford University Press, 1993.

Fletcher Marvin E. *The Black Soldier and Officer in the United States Army, 1891-1917.* Columbia, MO: University of Missouri Press, 1974.

_____*America's First Black General.* Lawrence, KS: University of Kansas Press, 1989.

Flipper, Henry O. *The Colored Cadet at west Point.* New York: Homer Lee & Co., 1878.

_____ *Negro Frontiersman.* El Paso, TX: Texas Western Press, 1963

Fogel, Robert W., and Stanley L. Engerman. *Time on the Cross.* Boston: Little, Brown and Company, 1974.

Foner, Eric. *Nothing But Freedom.* Baton Rouge, LA: Louisiana State University Press, 1983•1988,

_____ *Reconstruction. 1863-1877.* New York: Harper & Row,

Franklin, John H. and Alfred A. Moss, Jr. *From Slavery to Freedom.* New York: Knopf, 1994.

Fredrickson, George M. *The Arrogance of Race.* Hanover NH :Wesleyan University Press, 1988.

_____Honover NH .Wesleyan University Press, 1971.

Genovese, Eugene D. *Roll. Jordan. Roll.* New York: Vintage Books, 1874.

Glathaar, Joseph T. *Forged in Battle.* New York: Free Press, 1990.

Gooding, Corporal James Henry. *On the Altar of Freedom.* Amherst, MA: University of Massachusetts Press, 1991.

Hoffer, Eric. *The Temper of our Time.* New York: Harper & Row, 1964.

Hurst, Jack. *Nathan Bedford Forrest.* New York: Knopf, 1993.

Isaacs, Harold R. *The New World of Negro Americans.* New York: The John Day Company, 1963.

Johnson, Robert and Clarence Buel, eds. *Battles and Leaders of the Civil War.* New York: The Century Company, 1889.

Jones, Jacqueline. *Soldiers of Light and Love.* Athens, GA: University of Georgia Press, 1992.

Katz, William L. *The Black West.* New York: Doubleday & Co, 1971.

Korngold, Ralph. *Thaddeus Stevens.* New York: Harcourt, Brace and Co., 1955.

Lanning, Michael L. *The African American Soldier.* Secaucus, NJ: Birch Lane Press, 1997.

Leckie, William H. *The Buffalo Soldiers.* Norman, OK: The University of Oklahoma Press, 1967.

Lewis, David L. *W.E.B. DuBois Biography of a Race.* New York: Henry Holt & Co., 1993.

Litwack, Leon F. *Been in the Sore So Long.*. New York: Random House, 1979.

Logan, Rayford W. *Howard University: the First Hundred Years.* New York: New York University Press, 1969.

Loye, David. *The Healing of a Nation.* New York: W.W.. Norton & Co, 1971.

Marszalek, John F. *Court-Martial.* New York: Scribner's, 1972.

_____*Sherman.* New York: Free Press, 1993.

McFeely, Williams. *Frederick Douglass.* New York: W.W. Norton & Co, 1991.

McPherson, James M. *Ordeal by Fire.* New York; McGraw Hill, Second Edition, 1992.

_____*The Abolitionist Legacy.* Princeton, NJ: Princeton University Press, 1975.

_____*The Negro's Civil War.* New York: Ballantine, 1965

_____*The Struggle for Equality.* Princeton, NJ: Princeton University Press, 1964.

Meier, August. *Negro Thought in America. 1880-1915.* Ann Arbor, MI: University of Michigan Press, 1963.

Meltzer, Milton, ed. *The Black Americans, a History in Their Own Words, 1619-1983.* New York: Harper & Row, 1984.

Miller, William L. *Arguing About Slavery.* New York: Knopf, 1996.

Morison, Samuel E., Henry S. Commager, and William E. Leuchtenburg. *The Growth of the American Republic.* sixth Edition, New York: Oxford University Press, 1969.

Myrdal, Gunnar. *An American Dilemma: The Negro Problem and Modern Democracy.* New York: Harper & Brothers, 1944

Nalty, Bernard C.. *Strength for the Fight; a History of Black Americans in the Military.* New York: Free Press, 1986.

Nalty, Bernard C. and Morris J. McGregor. *Blacks in the Military: Essential Documents.* Wilmington, DE: Scholarly Resources, 1981.

Paret, Peter, ed. *Makers of Modern Strategy.* Princeton, NJ: Princeton University Press, 1986.

Parish, Peter J. *Slavery. History and Historians.* New York: Harper & Row, 1989.

Quarles, Benjamin. *The Negro in the Making of America.* New York: Collier Books, 1964.

Ransom, Roger L. and Richard Sutch. *One Kind of Freedom.* New York: Cambridge University Press, 1977.

Rudolph, Frederick. *The American College and University.* New York: Knopf, 1992.

Sears, Stephen. George B, McClellan. *The Young Napoleon.* New York: Harper & Row, 1988.

Stampp,, Kenneth M. *The Peculiar Institution; Slavery in the Antebellum South.* New York: Vintage Books, 1956.

Tocqueville, Alexis de. *Democracy in America.* New York: Phillips Bradley text, 1990.

Weigley, Russel F. *History of the United States Army.* Bloomington, IN-: University of Indiana Press, 1984.

Woodward, C. Vann. *The Strange Career of Jim Crow.* 3rd Ed., New York: Oxford University Press, 1974.

Zilversmit, Arthur. *The First Emancipation:The Abolition of Slavery in the North.* Chicago: University of Chicago Press, 1967.

Essays

Akers, Frank H. "They Fought for the Union and Equality: Blacks in the Civil War." *Army* 25 (March 1975): 47-51.

Bailey, Sedell. "Buffalo Soldiers." *Armor* 83 (January/February 1974): 9-12.

Branley, Bill. "Black, White & Red: A Story of Black Cavalrymen in the West." *Soldiers* 36 (June 1981): 44-48.

Butler, Johns and Malcolm D. Holmes. "Perceived Discrimination and the Military Experience." *Journal of Political and Military Sociology* 9: (Spring 1981): 17-30

Cornish, Dudley T. "To Be Recognized as Men: The Practical Utility of Military History." *Military Review* 58 (February 1978):40-55.

Fincher, Jack. "The Hard Fight Was Getting into the Fight at All." *Smithsonian* 21 (1990): 46-61.

Friedrich, Otto. "We Will Not Do Duty Any Longer For Seven Dollars Per Month." *American Heritage* 39 (1988): 64-73.

Gatewood, Eillard B. Jr. "John Hanks Alexander of Arkansas: Second Black Graduate of West Point." *Arkansas Historical Quarterly* 41 (1982): 103-128.

Heinl, Nancy G. "Col. Charles Young, Pointman." *Army* 27 (March 1977): 30-33.

Janowitz, Morris and Charles c. Moskos, Jr. "Racial Composition in the All-Volunteer Force." *Armed Forces and Society* 1 (November 1974): 109-123.

Mann, JoAnn. "Black Americans in the War for Independence." *Soldiers* 30 (January 1975): 30-35.

Marszalek, John F., Jr. "Black Man in Military History." *Negro History Bulletin* 36 (October 1873): 122.

Michie, William S. "Caste at West Point." *North American Review*, Vol. CXXX (June 1880): 604-618.

Miles, Donna. "They Ranged the Old West as Buffalo Soldiers." *Soldiers* 45 (July 1990): 42-44.

Modell, John, Marc Goulden, and Sigurder Magnusson. "World War II in the Lives of Black Americans: Some Findings and an Interpretation." *Journal of American History* 76 (1989): 838-848.

Moskos, Charles c. Racial Integration in the Army. *Army* 16 (August 1966): 50-54.

Smith, A. Wade. "Public Consciousness of Blacks in the Military." *Journal of Political and Military Sociology* 11 (Fall 1983): 281-300.

Spencer, Rainier H. "Blacks, the Army and America." *Military Review* 72 (July 1992): 3-9.

Spiller, Roger J. "Honoring the Buffalo Soldiers." *American Heritage* 43 (February-March 1992): 84-85.

Vaughn, William P. "West Point and the First Negro Cadet." *Military Affairs*, Vol. XXXV No.3 (October 1971):

White, James S. "Race Relations in .the Army." *Military Review* 50 (July 1970): 3-12.

Wilson, Steve. "A Black Lieutenant in the Ranks." *American History Illustrated* 18 (1983): 31

Government Publications

Byers, Jean. *A study of the Negro in Military Service*. Washington, DC: Department of Defense, 1950.

Lee, Ulysses G. *The Employment of Negro Troops*. U.S.. Army Center of Military History, Washington, DC, 1994.

MacGregor, Morris J. Jr. *Integration of the Armed Forces 1940- 1965.* U.S. Army Center of Military History, Washington, DC, 1989.

American Military History. Washington, DC: U.S. Army Center of Military History, 1989.

Black Americans in Defense of our Nation. Department of Defense publication, U.S. Government Printing Office, Washington, D.C.., 1990.

Proceedings, In the Case of Henry O. Flipper (Deceased), U.S. Army Board for Correction of Military Records, 17 November. 1976.

Regulations for the U.S. Military Academy at West Point. New York: Baldwin and Jones, 1868.

Unpublished Dissertations and Theses

Andrews, Richard L., "Years of Frustration: William T. Sherman, the Army, and Reform, 1869-1883." Unpublished Ph.D. dissertation, Northwestern University, 1968.

Denton, Edgar III, "The Formative Years of the United States Military Academy, 1775-1833." Unpublished Ph.D. dissertation, Syracuse University, 1964.

Dillard, Walters., "The United States Military Academy, 1865- 1900: the Uncertain Years." Unpublished Ph.D. dissertation, University of Washington, 1972.

Harris, Theodore D., "Henry Ossian Flipper, the First Negro Graduate of West Point." Unpublished Ph.D. dissertation, University of Minnesota, 1971.

Morrison, James L. Jr., "The United states Military Academy, 1833-1866: Years of Progress and Turmoil." Unpublished Ph.D. dissertation, Columbia University, 1970.

Phillips, Tom G., "The Black Regulars: Negro Soldiers in the United States Army, 1866-1891." Unpublished Ph.D. dissertation, University of Wisconsin, 1970.

Street, William B., Joseph Silbert, Dean of Engineering Emeritus at Cornell University, "Military Enterprise and Engineering Education: the American Experience", Cornell University., 1996.

Appendix A

Blacks Nominated for Appointment to the U.S. Military Academy in 19th Century

Nominee	Date(s) of Nomination	Nominating Official, Congressional District and State From Which Nominated
Charles Sumner Wilson	Mar. 7, 1870	Rep. Benjamin F. Butler 5th District, Mass.
Henry Alonzo Napier	Apr. 5, 1870	Rep. W.. F. Prosser 5th District, Tenn.
Michael Howard	Apr. 20, 1870 *Feb. 11, 1871	Rep. L.W. Perce 5th District, Miss.
James Webster Smith	May 23, 1870	Rep. S. L. Hoge 3d District, S.C..
James Elias Rector	Mar. 3, 1871	Rep. Thomas Boles 3d District, Ark.
Thomas Van Rensslear Gibbs	May 23, 1871	Rep. Josiah T. Walls 1n District, Fla.

Henry Ossian Flipper	Apr. 8, 1873	Rep. J. c. Freeman 5th District, Ga. Rep. J. H. Platt, Jr. 2d District, Va.
John Washington Williams	May 15, 1873	
William Henry Jarvis, Jr.	Feb. 3, 1874 *June 8, 1874	Rep. D.W. Gooch 5th District Mass.
William Henry White	Mar. 8, 1874 *June 12, 1874	Rep. Richard H. Cain At-Large, S.C.
Whitefield McKinlay	Mar. 25, 1874	Rep. A. J. Ransier 2d District, S C..
William Narcese Werles	Apr. 25, 1874	Rep. Albert R. Howe 2d District, Miss.
Johnson Chestnut Whittaker	May 24, 1876	Rep.S.. L. Hoge 3d District, S.C.
Joseph Thomas Dubuclet	Oct. 11, 1876	Rep. Charles E. Nash 6th District, La.
John Augustus Simkins	Jan. 30, 1877	Rep. Robert Smalls 5th District, S.C..
Charles Augustus Minnie	Aug. 23, 1877	Rep. Nicholas Muller 5th District, N.Y.
Lemuel W. Livingston	July 24, 1882	Rep. Horatio Bisbee, Jr. 2d District, Fla.
John Hanks Alexander	May 15, 1883	Rep. George W. Geddes 14th District, Ohio
Daniel Cato Sugg	Sept. 8, 1883	Rep. James E. O'Hara 2d District, N.C.
Robert Shaw Wilkinson	Jan. 15, 1884	Rep. E. W. M. Mackey 7tn District, S.C..
Charles Young	Apr. 29, 1884	Rep. Alphonso Hunt 12th District, Ohio
Julius Linoble Mitchell	July 23, 1884	Rep. Robert Smalls 7tn District, S.C.
William Trent Andrews	Aug. 27, 1884 *Oct. 8, 1884	Rep. Robert Smalls 7tn District, S.C.

Johns. Outlaw	Sept. 15, 1884 *May 1, 1885	Rep. James E. O'Hara 2d District, N.C.
William Achilles Hare	May 19, 1885	Rep. Martin A. Foran 21st District, Ohio
Henry Wilson Holloway	May 3, 1886 *July 9, 1886	Rep. Robert Smalls 7tn District, S.C..
Eli W.. Henderson	Mar. 2, 1887	Rep. Robert Smalls 7th District,S.C..

APPENDIX B

African-Americans Admitted to the U.S. Military Academy at West Point in 19th Century

Names	Date Admitted	Date of Separation	Reason for Separation
James Webster Smith	July 1, 1870		Def in Philosophy
Henry Alonzo Napier	July 1, 1871	June 30, 1872	Def, in Math & French
Thomas Van Rensselaer Gibbs	July 1, 1872	Jan. 11, 1873	Def. in Math
Henry Ossian Flipper	July l, 1873	June 15, 1877	Graduated
John Washington Williams	July 1, 1873	Jan. 19, 1874	Def. in French
Johnson Chestnut Whittaker	Sept. 1, 1876	Mar. 23, 1882	Def. in Philosophy
Charles Augustus Minnie	Sept. 1, 1877	Jan. 18, 1878	Def. in Math

John Hanks Alexander	July 1, 1883	June 12, 1887	Graduated
Charles Young	June 15, 1884	Aug. 31, 1889	Graduated
William Trent Andrews	June 14, 1885	Jan. 21, 1886	Def. in Math
William Achilles Hare	June 14, 1885	Jan. 21, 1886	Def. in Math, Eng., & Discipline
Henry Wilson Holloway	Sept. 1, 1886	Jan. 26, 1887	Def. in Math

CPSIA information can be obtained
at www.ICGtesting.com
Printed in the USA
BVHW032147240920
589611BV00001B/96